Mountain Biking
Oregon

Mark Wigg

FALCON®

HELENA, MONTANA

A **FALCON** GUIDE ®

Falcon® Publishing is continually expanding its list of recreation guidebooks. All books include detailed descriptions, accurate maps, and all the information necessary for enjoyable trips. You can order extra copies of this book and get information and prices for other Falcon guidebooks by writing Falcon, P.O. Box 1718, Helena, MT 59624 or calling toll free 1-800-582-2665. Also, please ask for a free copy of our current catalog. Visit our website at http://www.falconguide.com

© 1998 by Falcon® Publishing, Inc., Helena, Montana
Printed in the United States of America.

1 2 3 4 5 6 7 8 9 0 MG 03 02 01 00 99 98

Falcon and FalconGuide are registered trademarks of Falcon® Publishing, Inc.

All black-and-white photos by author unless otherwise noted.
Cover photo by Chuck Haney.

Library of Congress Cataloging-in-Publication Data
Wigg, Mark, 1952–
    Mountain biking Oregon / Mark Wigg.
      p. cm.
    ISBN 1-56044-671-4 (pbk. : alk. paper)
    1. All terrain cycling—Oregon—Guidebooks. 2. Oregon—Guidebooks.
I. Title.
GV1045.5.O7W55 1998
917.9504'43—dc21   98-29617
                                                CIP

CAUTION

Outdoor recreational activities are by their very nature potentially hazardous. All participants in such activities must assume the responsibility for their own actions and safety. The information contained in this guidebook cannot replace sound judgment and good decision-making skills, which help reduce risk exposure, nor does the scope of this book allow for disclosure of all the potential hazards and risks involved in such activities.

Learn as much as possible about the outdoor recreational activities in which you participate, prepare for the unexpected, and be cautious. The reward will be a safer and more enjoyable experience.

♻ Text pages printed on recycled paper.

Contents

Preface v

Map Legend vi

Statewide Locator Map vii

Introduction 1

Trail Park Permits 2
Climate 2
Riding Right! IMBA Rules of the Trail 3
How to Use this Guide 5
Rating the Rides 7
Aerobic Level Ratings 7
Technical Difficulty Ratings 8
Elevation Graphs 9

The Oregon Trail 10
   1 Barlow Road: Gate Creek to Government Camp 10
   2 Pioneer Bridle Trail 16

Portland 20
   3 Springwater Corridor: McLoughlin Boulevard to Gresham 20
   4 Springwater Corridor: Gresham to Boring 23
   5 Powell Butte Park 27
   6 Forest Park: Springville Road Loop 31

Oregon's Coast and Coast Range 36
   7 Banks/Vernonia State Park 37
   8 Gales Creek 41
   9 Nels Rogers: University Falls Loop Trail 43
 10 Bayocean Peninsula 45
 11 Mary's Peak 48
 12 McDonald Forest: Calloway Creek to Cap House Loop 51

Columbia River Gorge 56
 13 Tanner Creek Road 56
 14 Eagle Creek Overlook to Bonneville Dam 59
 15 Hood River to Mosier 61
 16 Sandy Delta 65

West Slope Cascades 69
 17 Shellrock Lake to Rock Lake Basin 69
 18 Indian Ridge/Shining Lake Trail 72
 19 Olallie Scenic Area Loop 74
 20 Mollala River 77
 21 Opal Creek 79

Willamette Valley 83

  22 Willamette Mission State Park 83
  23 E. E. Wilson Wildlife Area 86
  24 Row River Trail 89

Southwest Oregon 93

  25 Dunning Ranch.. 93
  26 North Umpqua Trail: Tioga Segment 96
  27 Crater Lake: East Entrance.. 102
  28 OC & E Woods Line State Trail: Bly to Klamath Falls 106
  29 OC & E Woods Line State Trail: Woods Line Branch 110

Central Oregon 116

  30 Hoodoo to Link Lake Loop 117
  31 Suttle Lake to Dark Lake 120
  32 Eagle Rock Loop 123
  33 Peterson Ridge Loop 125
  34 Snow Creek Loop 128
  35 Three Creeks Long Loop 131
  36 Swampy Lakes Loop 133
  37 Tumalo Falls 136
  38 Lava Lake to Sparks Lake: Trails 4 and 99 138
  39 Phil's Trail 24.5 141
  40 Deschutes River Trail: Lava Island to Benham Falls 143
  41 Lower Deschutes River Trail 146
  42 Davis Lake to Bobby Lake 149

Southeast Oregon 153

  43 Steens Mountain 153
  44 McCoy Ridge 156
  45 Tombstone Canyon 159

The Blue Mountains 162

  46 Lookout Mountain Trail 162
  47 Independent Mine Trail 165
  48 Round Mountain Trail... 167
  49 Cougar Creek Trail 169
  50 Imnaha River Trail 172

Appendix A 175
Appendix B 177

Preface

Mountain biking opportunities in Oregon have expanded exponentially in the last five years. The majority of Oregon's thirteen national forests now have mountain bike routes (lists of recommended rides are available from the Forest Service). There are also great rides on Bureau of Land Management (BLM) land. Between them, these two agencies manage about half the land in the state; land with more miles of backcountry road than all of the state's paved highways combined.

Recently, to protect fish and wildlife habitat, these agencies closed several thousand miles of backcountry road to automobiles. However, many of these closed roads are still open to biking. In addition, Oregon's Departments of Transportation, Parks, Forestry, and Fish and Wildlife have expanded mountain-biking opportunities in cooperation with many of the state's cities. Oregon now has so many riding opportunities that they can't all be described in a single book.

In selecting rides for this book, I looked for routes that had not been described in other mountain bike guides; some of these routes are so new, they won't be officially opened until after this book is published. A few of the rides were selected because of their historical significance—riding in ruts made by pioneer wagons 150 years ago adds a new dimension to mountain biking. Some rides were chosen for their exceptional scenic beauty and others for their wildlife. I tried to include rides for all skill levels; from easy rides for family outings, to rides that will challenge hard-core riders. The rides cover most of the state's geographic regions—from the coast to the high desert—and the appendices includes the addresses and phone numbers of agencies to contact for more information.

People do amazing things on bikes. I've seen people ride off cliffs, bunny-hop over jetty rocks, and do flips. Fortunately, you won't need to do any of those things to finish the rides in this book. I'm a middle-aged guy who follows this motto: When the riding gets really rough—and before it gets dangerous—get off and walk. Mountain biking can be exhilarating and exhausting; you can be laughing giddily on a downhill glide one moment, and cursing a brutally steep climb the next. You can go places that are off-limits to cars, yet too far to walk to in a day. With this book as your guide, you can use your mountain bike as a fun and interesting way to explore the beautiful backroads and trails of Oregon.

MAP LEGEND

Trail/Singletrack		Town	
Hiking Trail		City	
Doubletrack		Trailhead	
Paved Road		Alternate Trailhead	
Gravel Road		Route Marker	
Interstate		Parking	
Wilderness Boundary		Interstate	
Waterway		U.S. Highway	
Lake/Reservoir		State Highway	
Picnic Area		Forest Road	
Elevation		Gate	
Ride Locator		Building	
Orientation		Campground	
		Bridge	

Scale

0   0.5   1

MILES

Statewide Locator Map

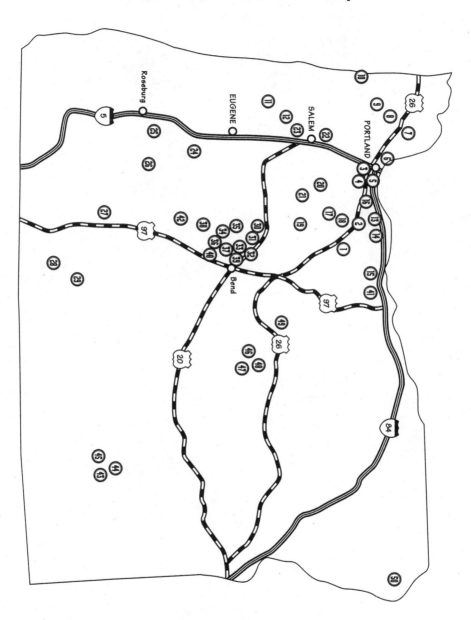

Introduction

This book is intended to help you choose a ride that is appropriate for your fitness and skill level, guide you to the trailhead, and make it easy for you to follow the trail. It gives tips on what to bring and provides background information about each area to make the rides more interesting.

The rides in this book cover varied terrain. Some are in the mountains, which means they are steep, rough, and subject to rapidly changing weather. At high altitudes, storms can roll in suddenly, bringing rain, hail, lightning and even snow, at any time of year. You must be prepared. Get in good shape before you attempt these rides, and know your limits. Keep your bike running smoothly with frequent cleaning and maintenance. Check to make sure that tires, rims, brakes, handlebars, seat, shifters, derailleurs, and chain are functioning properly before you start a ride—and preferably before you leave home.

For trips through remote areas (more than a mile from town) bring enough equipment to survive overnight. The essentials are:

1. A map, compass, and the ability to use them. The maps in this book won't help you if you're lost, because they cover such a small area.
2. A flashlight with good batteries.
3. A whistle; three blasts is the signal for help.
4. Extra clothing, including a waterproof, windproof jacket.
5. Extra food and water; I drink more than a gallon of water on long trips. Don't expect to find water at the trailhead.
6. A pocketknife.
7. Waterproof matches or lighter.
8. Fire starter such as a candle.
9. First aid kit.
10. Sunblock, sunglasses, and insect repellent.

Your repair kit should include:
1. Tire pump.
2. Tire patch kit. I also use thorn-guards inside the tires, flat-proof gels, and extra thick tubes.
3. Spare tube.
4. Allen wrenches for all the screws on the bike.
5. Vise-grip wrench.
6. Lubricant.
7. Duct tape.

Some folks recommend bringing a chain rivet tool, extra chain links, a spoke wrench, extra spokes, an air gauge, and extra nuts and bolts.

Good cycling gloves protect your hands from the cuts and bruises that can result from falls or encroaching branches and rocks; they also improve your grip and comfort on the handlebars. I also bring a plastic bag to pack out litter.

Check the weather conditions before you head for the trail, and call the appropriate managing agency to see if the trail is open. It is also a good idea to make your travel plans known to someone else.

Always wear a helmet; it can save your life.

TRAIL PARK PERMITS

The Willamette, Mt. Hood, Deschutes, Siuslaw, and Wallowa-Whitman national forests require day-use ($3) or seasonal ($25) permits to park near trailheads. The permits are available at many sporting goods stores or at Forest Service offices.

The money collected is used to maintain trails in the region. Trail budgets have not been adequate to maintain the trail system in recent years. The trailheads will be signed accordingly if permits are required. Ultimately, this program will improve trail maintenance and is worth supporting.

CLIMATE

Oregon's climate is determined by the complex interactions of continental and Pacific air masses moving back and forth across the mountain ranges. The moisture and moderate temperatures of the Pacific air mass keep the coast and Coast Range wet and snow-free. Sunny days and frost are rare events from November to March, and summer temperatures of more than 80 degrees F are infrequent. Winds are almost constant on the coast.

The Coast Range creates a modest rain shadow for the Willamette Valley. As a result, the valley is drier than the coast. Winters in the Willamette Valley are cloudy and mild with only a few days of snow each year and temperatures usually stay between 35 and 55 degrees F. Summer temperatures typically range from the low 70s to the high 80s, with a couple of weeks in the 90s. Summer thunderstorms and rain are infrequent.

The Cascades wring both rain and snow from Pacific storms before they move on to Central Oregon. The potential for dramatic weather changes requires that you be prepared for all types of weather. Snow can fall any day of the year, while summer highs may top 100 degrees F. In general, temperatures are cooler at higher elevations (by as much as 10 degrees F for every 1,000 feet gained). Take a variety of clothes to match the variable weather you may encounter. Most trails in the Cascades are closed due to snow from November to May.

As you descend the eastern slope of the Cascades, the annual precipitation drops from more than 100 inches at the crest to less than 10 inches in the deserts. At higher elevations in the Cascades, the trails may only be open from June to October, but trails in the lower Cascades and the deserts of Central Oregon may be open all year. Central Oregon is mountain biking heaven. With the Cascades blocking most of the rain and snow, the days are sunny, the scenery is varied and spectacular, and the trail network is extensive. Summer temperatures, moderated by Oregon's latitude and the Pacific, rarely exceed 100 degrees F. Snow sometimes prevents riding through the ponderosa pine forests, but the lower elevation roads through sage and juniper rarely receive snow. The sand and pumice surface of most roads and trails allows them to drain quickly and be suitable for riding on all but the wettest days. However, these trails may become impassibly soft by mid-summer. When this happens, you can head east to the Blue Mountains or the basin-and-range country, where road surfaces are harder.

The Blue Mountain geographic region, which includes the Ochoco, Wallowa, and Blue Mountain ranges, do not receive as much snow as the Cascades and, in general, they are not as rugged. The trails are usually open from May to November, depending on the elevation. In some years these routes are bare and rideable even in winter. Be aware, however, that even a brief rain or minor snowmelt can soften soils and leave trails vulnerable to erosion. Remember, a single bike tire can form a rut that channels runoff on the trail. Water eats at the rut and widens it into an erosion gully that can wipe out that route. Ruts also erode public acceptance of bikes on trails. Preventing both types of erosion is essential for preserving trail access for all mountain bikers.

The arid basin-and-range country of southeastern Oregon has 100-degree days in the summer and cold, dry winters. Thunderstorms are common. Trails at lower elevations may be free of snow year-round, but they turn to muck when wet.

RIDING RIGHT! IMBA RULES OF THE TRAIL

If every mountain biker always yielded the right-of-way, stayed on the trail, avoided wet or muddy trails, never cut switchbacks, never skidded, always rode in control, showed respect for other trail users, and carried out every last scrap of what was carried in (candy wrappers and bike-part debris included)—in short, *did the right thing*—then we wouldn't need a list of rules governing our behavior.

Most mountain bikers are conscientious and are trying to do the right thing. Most of us *own* that basic integrity. Most of us don't need rules, but we do need knowledge. What exactly is the right thing to do?

Here are some guidelines—think of them as reminders—reprinted by permission from the International Mountain Bicycling Association (IMBA). The basic theme here is reducing or eliminating impact on the land and water, the plant and wildlife inhabitants, and other backcountry visitors and trail users. Ride with respect.

IMBA Rules of the Trail

Thousands of miles of dirt trails have been closed to mountain bikers. The irresponsible riding habits of some riders have been a factor in many of these closures. Do your part to maintain trail access by observing the following rules of the trail, formulated by the International Mountain Bicycling Association (IMBA). IMBA's mission is to promote environmentally sound and socially responsible mountain biking.

3

1. Ride on open trails only. Respect trail and road closures (ask if not sure), avoid possible trespass on private land, and obtain permits and authorization as required. Federal and state wilderness areas are closed to cycling. The way you ride will influence trail management decisions and policies.

2. Leave no trace. Be sensitive to the dirt beneath you. Even on open (legal) trails, you should not ride when conditions will cause you to leave evidence of your passing, such as on certain soils after a rain. Recognize different types of soil and trail construction; practice low-impact cycling. This also means staying on existing trails and not creating any new ones. Be sure to pack out at least as much as you pack in.

3. Control your bicycle! Inattention for even a second can cause problems. Obey all bicycle speed regulations and recommendations.

4. Always yield trail. Make your approach known well in advance. A friendly greeting (or bell) is considerate and works well; don't startle others. Show your respect when passing by slowing to a walking pace or even stopping. Anticipate other trail users around corners or in blind spots.

5. Never spook animals. All animals are startled by an unannounced approach, a sudden movement, or a loud noise. This can be dangerous for you, others, and the animals. Give animals extra room and time to adjust to you. When passing horses, use special care and follow directions from the horseback riders (ask if uncertain). Running cattle and disturbing wildlife is a serious offense. Leave gates as you found them, or as marked.

6. Plan ahead. Know your equipment, your ability, and the area in which you are riding—and prepare accordingly. Be self-sufficient at all times, keep your equipment in good repair, and carry necessary supplies for changes in weather or other conditions. A well-executed trip is a satisfaction to you and not a burden or offense to others. Always wear a helmet.

Keep trails open by setting a good example of environmentally sound and socially responsible cycling. In addition to the above guidelines, try to keep your riding group small and avoid using trails at the times of day or week that are heavily used by hikers and equestrians.

Consider joining one of the local groups working to maintain and create trails. Some of the most active trail groups are equestrian clubs. Find out when they are having a work party and work with them. Become more involved in helping city and county officials plan and develop open space. Get involved with the road closure program in the National Forests and BLM Districts and identify roads that would make good bike trails. Become an advocate for trails.

HOW TO USE THIS GUIDE

Mountain Biking Oregon describes fifty mountain bike rides in their entirety and offers more than a dozen alternate routes. Many of the featured rides are loops, beginning and ending at the same point, but coming and going on different trails. Loops are by far the most popular type of ride.

Be forewarned, however: the difficulty of a loop ride may change dramatically depending on which direction you ride around the loop. If you are unfamiliar with the rides in this book, try them first as described here. The directions follow the path of least resistance (which does not necessarily mean "easy"). After you've been over the terrain, you can determine whether a given loop would be fun—or even feasible—in the reverse direction.

Portions of some rides follow gravel and, occasionally, paved roads; a few rides never even wander off road at all. Purists may wince at road rides in a book about mountain biking, but these are special rides. They offer a chance for people new to the sport to enjoy mountain scenery and fresh air while covering easier, non-technical terrain. They can also be used by hard-core riders when higher elevation trails are closed by mud or snow.

Each ride description in this book follows the same format, beginning with the **number and name of the ride:** Rides are cross-referenced by number throughout this book. In many cases, parts of rides or entire routes can be linked to other rides for longer trips or variations on a standard route. These opportunities are duly noted. For the names of rides, I relied on official names of trails, roads, and natural features as shown on U.S. Geological Survey maps. Some of the trails are new and are not shown on these USGS maps.

The name and number of the ride are followed by an **overview** section. This brief text describes the plant communities, historical aspects, wildlife, and scenery you may encounter on the route. It also gives a brief description of the ride.

After the overview, the following headings provide the reader/rider with quick access to easy-to-understand information:

General location: The general location of the ride with distance and direction from the nearest town.
Distance: The length of the ride in miles, plus its configuration: loop, one way, or out-and-back.
Time: An estimate of how long it takes to complete the ride (for example, 1 to 2 hours). *The time listed is the actual riding time and does not include rest*

stops. Strong, skilled riders may be able to do a given ride in less than the estimated time; other riders may take considerably longer. Severe weather, changes in trail conditions, or mechanical problems may prolong a ride.

Aerobic level: The level of physical effort required to complete the ride, rated as easy, moderate, or strenuous. (See the explanation of the rating systems on page 7.)

Elevation change: An estimate of the total elevation gain on the ride.

Tread: The type of road or trail: paved road, gravel road, dirt road, doubletrack, or singletrack.

Technical difficulty: The level of bike handling skills needed to complete the ride upright and in one piece. Technical difficulty is rated on a scale from 1 to 5, with 1 being the easiest. (See the explanation of the rating systems on page 8.)

Hazards: A list of some of the dangers that may be encountered on a ride, including traffic, weather, and trail. Remember that conditions may change at any time. Be alert for storms, downfall, missing trail signs, and mechanical failure. Fatigue, heat, cold, and/or dehydration may impair judgment. Always wear a helmet and other safety equipment. Ride in control at all times.

Season: The time of year the trail may be open and/or the best time to ride.

Services: Identifies the nearest town with food, lodging, gas, and/or a phone.

Rescue Index: Suggests places to contact if you need help.

Land status: A list of managing agencies or landowners. All of the rides in this book are on public land. In some cases, the public right of way is the width of the trail; leaving the trail is trespassing. Respect private property. See Appendix A for phone numbers and addresses of land managing agencies.

Maps: A list of available maps. Many routes, but not all, are shown on official maps.

Sources of additional information: Provides the name of the land managing agency and suggests other maps and books that may provide information about the route.

Finding the trail: Detailed directions to the trailhead or the start of the ride.

The ride: Lists major features of the ride, such as landmarks, notable climbs and descents, stream crossings, obstacles, hazards, major turns, and junctions with other trails and roads. Terrain, riding technique, and even tire pressure can affect odometer readings, so treat all mileages as estimates.

Finally, one last reminder that the real world is changing all the time: The information presented here is as accurate and up-to-date as possible, but there are no guarantees. You alone are responsible for your safety and the safety of your party.

If you do find an error or omission in this book, or a new and noteworthy change in the field, we'd like to hear from you. Please write to Falcon Publishing, P.O. Box 1718, Helena, MT 59624.

RATING THE RIDES: ONE PERSON'S PAIN IS ANOTHER PERSON'S PLEASURE

One of the first lessons learned by most mountain bikers is to not trust their friends' accounts of how easy or difficult a given ride may be.

"Where ya wanna ride today?"

"Let's do 'The Wall,' dudes—it's gnarly in the middle, but even my grandma could fly up that last hill, and the view is way cool."

If you don't read between the lines, only painful experience will tell you that granny won the pro-elite class in last weekend's hillclimb race and "the view" is over the handlebars from the lip of a 1,000-foot drop on that fun little gnarly stretch.

So how do you know what you're getting into, before it's too late?

Read this book, contact the managing agencies and talk to folks at the local bike sops. This guide rates each ride for two types of difficulty: the physical effort required to pedal the distance, and the level of bike-handling skills needed to stay upright and make it home in one piece. These sections are called **aerobic level** and **technical difficulty**. What follows is an explanation of the various ratings and what they mean.

AEROBIC LEVEL RATINGS

Bicycling is often touted as a relaxing, low-impact, and relatively easy way to burn excess calories and maintain a healthy heart and lungs. Mountain biking tends to pack a little more work (and excitement) into the routine.

Fat tires and soft (or rough) trails increase the rolling resistance, so it takes more effort to push those wheels around. Unpaved or off-road hills tend to be steeper than grades measured and tarred by the highway department. When we use the word steep, we mean a sweat-inducing, oxygen-sucking climb. Expect to breathe hard and sweat some, probably a lot.

Pedaling around town is a good start, but it won't fully prepare you for the workout offered by the more difficult rides in this book. If you're unsure of your level of fitness, see a doctor for a physical exam before tackling any of these rides. If you're riding to get back in shape or just for the fun of it, take it easy. Walk or rest if need be. Start with short rides and add miles gradually.

Here's how we rate the exertion level for terrain covered in this book:

Easy: Flat or gently rolling terrain. No steep sections or prolonged climbs. Most riders cruise in the big chainrings up front on "easy" terrain.

Moderate: Some hills. Climbs may be short and fairly steep or long and gradual. Most riders shift into their middle chainrings up front on "moderate" terrain.

Strenuous: Frequent or prolonged climbs steep enough to require riding in the smallest chainring up front, probably in the lowest gear. "Strenuous" terrain requires a high level of aerobic fitness, power, and endurance (typically acquired through many hours of riding and proper training). Less fit riders may need to dismount and walk.

Many rides are mostly easy and moderate but may have short strenuous sections. Other rides are mostly strenuous and should be attempted only after a complete medical checkup and implant of a second heart. Also, be aware that flailing through a highly technical section can be exhausting even on the flats. Good riding skills and a relaxed stance on the bike save energy. Some rides in this book are on easy terrain but are listed as moderate or strenuous because of their length.

Any ride can be strenuous if you ride it hard and fast. Conversely, the pain of a lung-burning climb grows easier to tolerate as your fitness level improves. Learn to pace yourself and rest before you are completely exhausted. Accidents are more likely to occur if you are exhausted. You won't think as clearly and are more susceptible to hypothermia if you are soaked with sweat and exhausted.

TECHNICAL DIFFICULTY RATINGS

While you're pushing up that steep, strenuous slope, wondering how much longer your burning lungs will last, remember that this pain may not be the only hurdle on the way to the top of the mountain. Fallen trees (downfall) may block the trail, it may be covered with cobbles, or it may narrow to a trace requiring careful wheel placement to negotiate. Save enough energy to maintain control of your bike and get back safely.

Mountain bikes will roll over or through an amazing array of challenges, but sometimes we older and wiser bikers get off our bikes and walk—*before* we flip over the handlebars. The foolhardy and young might say we have no sense of adventure. They hop onto their bikes with only the dimmest inkling of what lies ahead and brag about the "ride to hell" (leaving out the part about carrying their bikes half the distance because hell has some highly technical terrain). Cuts, bruises, and broken bones may be badges of courage for some, but I have no need to collect more of those badges. The tattooed and pierced set will find plenty of challenging rides in this book, but you don't need to be 20-something to enjoy mountain biking.

The technical difficulty ratings in this book help take the worst surprises out of backcountry rides. In the privacy of your own home you can make an honest appraisal of your bike handling skills, then find rides in these pages that are within your ability.

We rate technical difficulty on a scale from 1 to 5, from easiest to most difficult. We tried to make the ratings as objective as possible by considering the type of obstacles and the frequency of occurrence. The same standards were applied consistently through all the rides in this book.

Level 1: Smooth tread; road or doubletrack with no obstacles, ruts, or steeps. Requires basic bike riding skills.
Level 2: Mostly smooth tread; wide, well-groomed singletrack or road/doubletrack with minor ruts or loose gravel or sand.
Level 3: Irregular tread with some rough sections of single or doubletrack with obvious route choices and some steep sections. Occasional obstacles may include small rocks, roots, water bars, ruts, loose gravel or sand, and sharp turns or broad, open switchbacks.

Level 4: Rough tread with few smooth places; singletrack or rough doubletrack with limited route choices and steep sections, some with obstacles. Obstacles are numerous and varied, including rocks, roots, branches, ruts, sidehills, narrow tread, loose gravel or sand, and switchbacks.

Level 5: Continuously broken, rocky, root-infested, or trenched tread; singletrack or extremely rough doubletrack with few route choices and frequent, sudden, or severe changes in gradient. Some slopes are so steep that wheels lift off the ground; obstacles are nearly continuous and may include boulders, logs, water, large holes, deep ruts, ledges, piles of loose gravel, steep sidehills, encroaching trees, and tight switchbacks.

ELEVATION GRAPHS

An elevation profile accompanies each ride description to help you determine how easy or hard the ride is based on the elevation gain and loss. It is a good idea to weigh other factors too, such as elevation above sea level, total trip distance, weather and wind, and current trail conditions.

Again, most of the rides in this book cover varied terrain, with an ever-changing degree of technical difficulty. Some trails are smooth, with only occasional obstacles, while other trails are seemingly all obstacles. The path of least resistance is where you find it. In general, most obstacles are more challenging if you encounter them when you're climbing. On the other hand, the risk of flying over the handlebars is greater when descending.

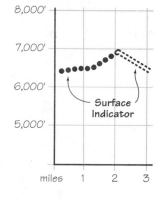

Realize, too, that different riders have different strengths and weaknesses. Some folks can scramble over logs and boulders without a grunt, but they crash head over heels on every switchback turn. Some fly off the steepest drops and others freeze. Some riders climb like the wind and others just blow . . . and walk.

The key to overcoming "technical difficulties" is practice: keep trying. Follow a rider who makes it look easy, and don't hesitate to ask for constructive criticism. Try shifting your weight (good riders move a lot, front to back, side to side, and up and down) and experimenting with balance and momentum. Find a smooth patch of lawn and practice riding as slowly as possible, even balancing at a standstill. This will give you more confidence—and more time to recover or bail out.

The Oregon Trail

The Oregon Trail brought thousands of people to the Willamette Valley in the 1800s. Men, women, and barefoot children made the months-long journey across the arid plains to arrive at the foot of the Cascades in early autumn.

The first pioneers floated down the Columbia River from The Dalles through a treacherous series of rapids near Cascade Locks. The Columbia was a wild river; many pioneers lost all of their possessions and some lost their lives. The locks to bypass the rapids were not completed until 1896.

Joel Palmer and Sam Barlow heard that Indian trails crossed the south flank of Mt. Hood. In 1845, the two pioneers traveled south from The Dalles to find the route. Joel Palmer's memoirs recounts climbing part way up what is now called Palmer Glacier to survey the route. He was barefoot; those folks had tough feet. The route they found would become the most difficult segment of the Oregon Trail, but it was not as dangerous or costly as floating the Columbia. They were not able to get their wagons over the trail the first year due to the slow process of clearing a trail. Sam Barlow returned the following spring and created the Barlow Road. Thousands of wagons eventually made the journey over the route blazed by Barlow and Palmer.

The first two rides in this book follow the pioneers' trail; you can ride in ruts made by their wagons.

Barlow Road: Gate Creek to Government Camp

After traveling 2,000 miles across the desert, most of Oregon's pioneers rested in the meadow along Gate Creek before beginning their climb over the Cascades. In 1845, Sam Barlow and a small group of pioneers blazed a route along Indian trails, across the southern flank of Mt. Hood and into the lush Willamette Valley. The following year, the Oregon legislature allowed Mr. Barlow to construct a toll road on the route. The alternative to this difficult mountain crossing for pioneers on the Oregon Trail was to float the Columbia River through a treacherous series of rapids. The meadow along Gate Creek was the site of the first tollgate for the road. Between 1845 and

BARLOW ROAD Ride

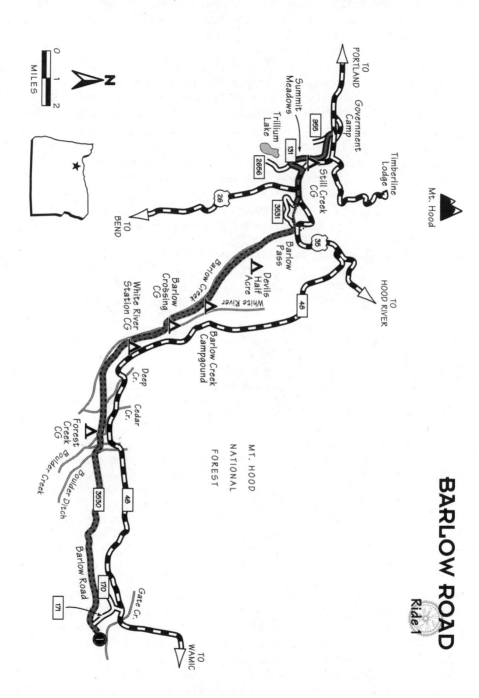

MT. HOOD NATIONAL FOREST

Mt. Hood

TO PORTLAND

Government Camp

Summit Meadows

955

Trillium Lake

131

2656

Timberline Lodge

Still Creek CG

26

TO BEND

3531

Barlow Pass

35

Devils Half Acre

Barlow Creek

White River

Barlow Crossing CG

White River Station CG

Barlow Creek Campgound

48

TO HOOD RIVER

Deep Cr.

Cedar Cr.

Forest Creek CG

Boulder Creek

Boulder Ditch

3530

48

Barlow Road

170

Gate Cr.

171

TO WAMIC

N

MILES
0 1 2

1910, more than two hundred thousand pioneers used this route. The graves of a few pioneers who did not survive the trek are marked along the road near Barlow Pass and Summit Meadows. The road was managed as a private toll road until 1918.

Ruts from the wagons are still visible on the steep hillsides where the pioneers lowered their wagons on ropes. This road is the longest, most primitive portion of the Oregon Trail open for public travel. To appreciate the historic significance of this route, read some of the pioneers' diaries before riding from east to west. You may want to take a few days to camp along the trail at the sites used by the pioneers. Most of the route has a gradual grade, smooth tread, and is suitable for family riding trips. Starting at Government Camp and riding to Gate Creek is an easier one-way ride.

General location:	In northwest Oregon, 11 miles southwest of Wamic near the eastern boundary of the Mt. Hood National Forest.
Distance:	24.4 miles, one way.
Time:	5 to 6 hours.
Aerobic level:	Strenuous.
Elevation change:	Gate Creek is 1,940 feet below Government Camp, but the trail climbs an additional 1,000 feet, passing in and out of river canyons.
Tread:	Dirt road; short segments of singletrack and paved road.
Technical difficulty:	2; some sections of 3.
Hazards:	Watch for other trail users, including motorized vehicles. Short segments are steep and rocky. The trail is slippery when wet.
Season:	May through October.
Services:	Government Camp and Wamic have most services.
Rescue index:	Help is available in Government Camp and Wamic.
Land status:	Barlow, Bear Springs, and Zigzag ranger districts of Mt. Hood National Forest; Oregon Department of Fish and Wildlife.
Maps:	Mt. Hood National Forest recreation map; Bear Springs Ranger District map. USGS: Wamic, Rock Creek Reservoir, Post Point, Wapanitia Pass, Badger Lake, Mt. Hood South.

Sources of additional information: Most libraries in Oregon have books about the Oregon Trail and Barlow Road. The most interesting accounts are the diaries of the pioneers. The Mt. Hood National Forest office in Sandy and the Oregon Trail Museum in Oregon City are also good sources of information.

Finding the trail: Take Forest Road 48 (a two-lane paved road) about 8.5 miles west of Wamic, or 20 miles south of Oregon 35, to FR 170 (the junction of OR 35 and FR 48 is about 7 miles east of Government Camp). Follow gravel FR 170 south from FR 48 about 0.3 mile, to its junction with FR 171. FR 171 is the second road on the left after leaving FR 48. Follow FR 171

Hell's Half-Acre on the Barlow Road.

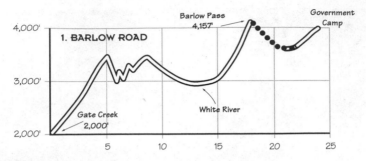

Barlow Pass
4,157'

Government
Camp

4,000'

1. BARLOW ROAD

3,000'

Gate Creek
2,000'

White River

2,000'

5   10   15   20   25

about 1 mile through pine and oak until it hits the Barlow Road (FR 3530) at the edge of a large meadow. Turn east (left) on the dirt road and proceed for 0.1 mile to a green gate. Park off the road near the green gate. The site of the Barlow Road's eastern tollgate is 0.5 mile past the green gate, in a meadow near a large cottonwood. The 120 acres surrounding the tollgate site is part of the White River State Game Management Area.

THE RIDE

From Gate Creek and the edge of the desert, climb gradually on the Barlow Road (Forest Road 3530) through oak, ponderosa pine, and Douglas-fir forests. In addition to the standard Forest Service road signs, the trail is marked at regular intervals with cedar posts emblazoned with a triangular trail logo. Several interpretive signs along the road provide insight into the trail's history.

Ride past several campgrounds that were campsites for the pioneers. After climbing for 6 miles, you drop into the Boulder Creek canyon. The road then climbs over ridges and into Cedar Creek and Deep Creek canyons before reaching the White River. Continue on the Barlow Road along the glacial milk–colored White River for about 4 miles before turning west to follow Barlow Creek to Barlow Pass. A large parking lot at Barlow Pass has an interpretive sign and is the start of a singletrack that follows the wagon trail down to the East Fork Salmon River crossing.

The steep singletrack ends at FR 3531. Continue west on FR 3531, past the Pioneer Woman's Grave to Oregon Highway 35. Follow OR 35 west, past its junction with U.S. Highway 26, and turn onto FR 2656, which has signs for Trillium Lake. About 0.1 mile down FR 2656, a cedar post marks the original route of the Barlow Road. This section is not maintained and is difficult to follow through the swamp of Summit Meadows.

Avoid the swamp by staying on FR 2656 to its junction with FR 131, which heads north to Summit Meadows and Still Creek Campground. Climb west from Still Creek Campground on a rocky trail (the only trail heading west from the campground). Follow this rough section of the Barlow Road to the Forest Service Guard Station on FR 955, and across U.S. 26 to Government Camp.

Knee deep in Summit Meadows near the Barlow Road.

Pioneer Bridle Trail

This exhilarating descent tests your brakes and forearm strength more than your legs. The construction of U.S. Highway 26 obliterated large sections of the Barlow Road west of Government Camp, but this trail follows the general route. The trail ends at the Barlow Road Tollgate, which was in service from 1883 to 1918. The gate is a reconstruction, but one of the original gatekeepers planted the maple trees that are now on either side of the gate in the 1800s. The upper trail passes through fir forests. The lower trail winds through lodgepole pines and over rocky glacial and riverine deposits. The infrequent but spectacular views of Mt. Hood and the Zigzag Valley are easy to miss as you try to control your descent.

General location:	The trail runs between Government Camp and Rhododendron in northwest Oregon.
Distance:	9.2 miles, one way.
Time:	1 to 2 hours.
Aerobic level:	Moderate.
Elevation change:	1,800-foot descent.
Tread:	This dirt and rock singletrack is in fair condition near Government Camp, but it becomes a wide, cobble-covered rut for long stretches after crossing U.S. Highway 26.
Technical difficulty:	4.
Hazards:	Equestrians, hikers, and cyclists are frequently encountered. Always maintain control and be prepared to yield to other trail users. Crossing U.S. Highway 26 is hazardous, especially on weekends when the stream of traffic is unbroken.
Season:	The trail is open between May and November; ride it only when it is dry.
Services:	Rhododendron and Government Camp have most services.
Rescue index:	Help is available in Government Camp and Rhododendron.
Land status:	Mt. Hood National Forest, Zigzag Ranger District.
Maps:	Mt. Hood National Forest publishes a recreation map, but the Zigzag Ranger District map provides more detail. USGS: Government Camp, Rhododendron.

Sources of additional information: The Forest Service Visitor Center in Mt. Hood Village, west of Welches.

Finding the trail: The Glacier View Sno-park, north of U.S. Highway 26, provides access to the trail. The Sno-Park is about 0.5 miles west of the western

PIONEER BRIDLE TRAIL
Ride 2

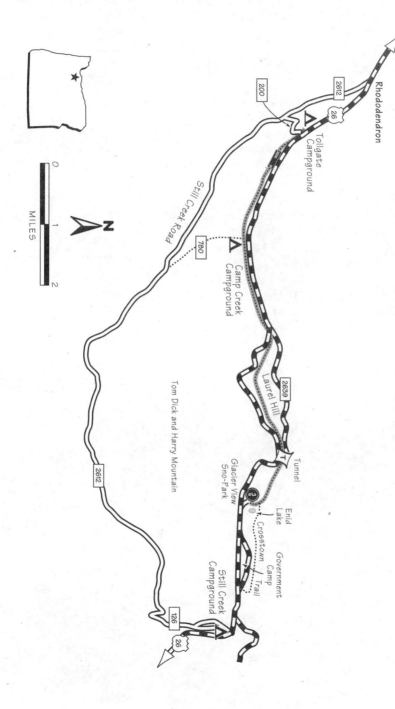

Rhododendron

2612

26

200

Toligate Campground

Still Creek Road

780

Camp Creek Campground

2639

Laurel Hill

Tunnel

Glacier View Sno-Park

Enid Lake

Government Camp

Crosstown Trail

Still Creek Campground

Tom Dick and Harry Mountain

2612

126

26

MILES

0   1   2

N

entrance to Government Camp. You can also access the trail in Government Camp by taking the road near Summit Ski area to the Crosstown Trail and following the Crosstown Trail west.

THE RIDE

Leave your shuttle car at the Tollgate Historic Site, 0.7 mile east of Rhododendron. From Glacier View Snopark, the trail begins a rapid descent. Keep to the left when passing the trails to Enid Lake and Government Camp. About 1.5 miles down the trail, you pass through a tunnel under the old highway, which is now Forest Road 2639. (If you want to avoid the steepest part of the Bridle Trail, get on FR 2639 at the tunnel and follow it down to U.S. Highway 26. The Bridle Trail

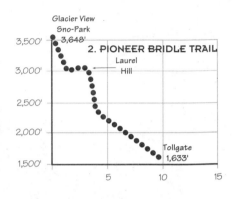

and FR 2639 meet US 26 at about the same location.) Shortly after the tunnel, a steep side trail drops to the right. Keep to the left to stay on the

Bob Carson at Tollgate on the Pioneer Bridle Trail.

Pioneer Bridle Trail. After a series of switchbacks, the trail crosses US 26. This crossing is hazardous, so use extreme caution! The trail parallels the highway, occasionally widening to road width. The trail crosses several forest roads, but continue riding parallel to the highway to stay on the trail. The trail is forced back onto the shoulder of the highway for 100 yards when it reaches several summer homes. The shoulder is wide enough at this point to ride it safely. The trail ends at the western tollgate to the Barlow Road.

Loop alternative: The Forest Service recommends a 20-mile loop that starts at Camp Creek Campground, 2.5 miles east of Rhododendron. From the campground, follow Trail 780 until it meets Still Creek Forest Road 2612. The route climbs east on FR 2612 for 8 miles until it reaches the junction with FR 126. Take FR 126 through Still Creek Campground to U.S. Highway 26. Turn west on US 26 and proceed to Glacier View Sno-park. The cobble surface of the lower reaches of the Bridle Trail makes uphill travel almost impossible, so use this alternative route if you don't have a shuttle car.

Portland

Portland is home to thousands of mountain bikers who are fortunate to have dozens of singletrack trails within a two-hour drive. Rain and snow close most mountain trails in the Portland area to mountain biking for about six months every year, which is why many of the Portland-area trails I've chosen for this book are at relatively low altitudes, and are therefore suitable for riding during wet weather. The wet-weather rides are usually not singletracks, but most are closed to motorized vehicles.

Forest Park, in northwest Portland, a couple of miles from downtown, is the most popular mountain biking area in the city. Its trails, on the northeast slope of the Tualatin Mountains, challenge riders of all skill levels. The 1,000-foot climb from the Willamette River to Skyline Drive is a strain for any rider.

Cyclists looking for a more relaxed ride can explore 11-mile Leif Erikson Drive; or, in east Portland, ride the Springwater Corridor along Johnson Creek on a converted rail line for more than 16 miles. The Springwater Corridor caters to those seeking a less challenging ride, but provides access to several interesting parks. The Springwater Corridor connects to the trails in Powell Butte Park, which is a destination for riders seeking hills and singletracks. The Sandy River Delta at the northeastern edge of the Portland metropolitan area receives little use but offers some interesting terrain. The Forest Service acquired this area several years ago and its sandy trails can be explored even during the wettest weather.

Springwater Corridor: McLoughlin Boulevard to Gresham

From 1903 to 1958, the Springwater Corridor was one of the main routes for the Springwater Division Line, an electric railroad system in Portland which, at its peak, carried sixteen million passengers a year. The Springwater Division Line was acquired by the City of Portland in 1990, and its conversion from rail to trail was completed in 1996.

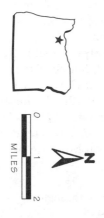

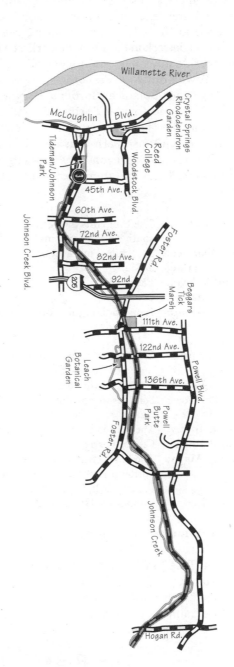

Willamette River

McLoughlin   Blvd.

Crystal Springs
Rhododendron
Garden

Reed
College

Woodstock Blvd.

Tideman/Johnson
Park

45th Ave.

60th Ave.

72nd Ave.

Foster Rd.

82nd Ave.

Johnson Creek Blvd.

92nd

205

Beggars
Tick
Marsh

111th Ave.

122nd Ave.

Leach
Botanical
Garden

136th Ave.

Powell Blvd.

Powell
Butte
Park

Foster Rd.

Johnson Creek

Hogan Rd.

N

MILES

0
1
2

The converted rail line runs past industrial districts, residential neighborhoods, shopping centers, forests, farms, and wetlands. While not a technical riding challenge, it is long enough to provide a good workout, especially if you add the 7.8-mile section from Gresham to Boring (see Ride 4). It also connects to several miles of singletrack in Powell Butte Park (see Ride 5). The Springwater Corridor is a good ride in winter, when few trails are open.

In addition to Powell Butte, several other parks are easily accessible from the trail, including Leach Botanical Gardens, Beggars Tick Marsh, Tideman-Johnson Nature Park, and Crystal Springs Rhododendron Garden. Riding the Springwater Corridor is a unique way to explore East Portland. The trail also connects to the multi-use path that parallels Interstate 205 between Vancouver, Washington, and Oregon City. The city has plans to extend the trail to the Willamette River and then north to the Oregon Museum of Science and Industry.

General location:	The trail runs along Johnson Creek, through the southern Portland metropolitan area.
Distance:	26.2 miles, out and back.
Time:	3 hours.
Aerobic level:	Easy.
Elevation change:	200 feet.
Tread:	From McLoughlin Boulevard through Gresham, the trail is paved.
Technical difficulty:	1.
Hazards:	The trail is heavily used on sunny weekends and has numerous driveway and street crossings.
Season:	The trail is open all year.
Services:	Services are available on cross streets along the entire trail.
Rescue index:	The trail is in the metropolitan area.
Land status:	City of Portland.
Maps:	The Springwater Corridor guide is available from the Portland Parks and Recreation Bureau. Most maps of the city still display the corridor as a railroad. USGS: Damascus, Gladstone.

Sources of additional information: Portland Parks and Recreation Bureau (see Appendix).

Finding the trail: Take Johnson Street Boulevard west from where it intersects with Interstate 205. The trailhead is located near the intersection of Johnson Creek Boulevard and 45th Street. Paved parking areas with restrooms are located at this trailhead and on Hogan Road in Gresham.

THE RIDE

If you park at the Johnson Creek Boulevard Trailhead, go west 0.5 mile to Tideman Johnson Park for a quick loop around the park on singletrack.

Watch for people and pets on the Springwater Corridor.

Continuing west on the Springwater Corridor for another 0.5 mile, you come to the end of the developed portion of the trail. Backtrack east for the long ride to Gresham. Trail use varies tremendously depending on the weather, time of day, and proximity to intersections. The trail becomes more rural after crossing I-205. The connecting trail to Powell Butte Park is signed and the park offers more strenuous and challenging singletracks.

Springwater Corridor: Gresham to Boring

The Gresham-to-Boring section of the Springwater Corridor is surprisingly secluded for being so close to a metropolitan area. It has fewer cross-streets than the section running from Gresham to McLoughlin. Early morning riders are likely to see a variety of wildlife, including deer, raccoons, herons, ducks, and coyotes. The ride begins near the Columbia Brick Works. This is Oregon's oldest operating brick manufacturer. The converted rail line crosses

SPRINGWATER CORRIDOR: GRESHAM TO BORING

Ride 4

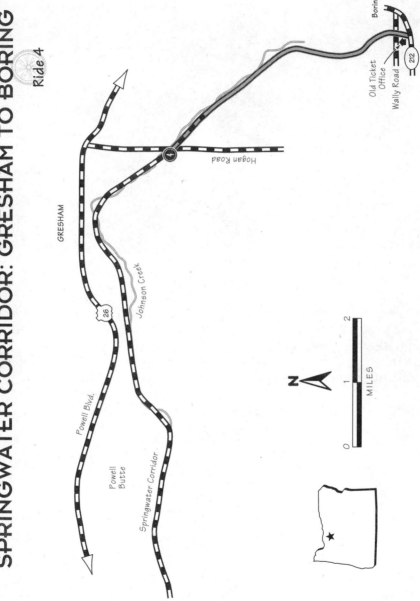

GRESHAM

Powell Blvd.

Powell Butte

Springwater Corridor

Johnson Creek

Hogan Road

26

4

Old Ticket Office

Wally Road

212

Boring

N

MILES

0   1   2

Johnson Creek a couple of times and passes through Douglas-fir forests, pastures, and farms before reaching Boring. Boring was named for W.H. Boring; the name was not meant to describe town life. The Springwater Corridor ends at the dilapidated depot in downtown Boring.

The 10-mile Cazadero Corridor between Boring and Estacada, which is ·managed by the Oregon State Parks Department, descends the forested Deep Creek Canyon, then runs along the Clackamas River past farms and forests to Estacada. With a little support from the public and politicians, the Parks Department may open the trail to bikers in a few years.

General location:	The trail begins in southeastern metropolitan Portland and runs along Johnson Creek from Gresham to Boring.
Distance:	7.8 miles, out and back.
Time:	1 hour.
Aerobic level:	Easy.
Elevation change:	Slight gain.
Tread:	The first mile from Hogan Road is paved, the rest is packed gravel.
Technical difficulty:	2.
Hazards:	The trail receives moderate use and has several driveway crossings.
Season:	The trail is open all year.
Services:	Services are available in Boring and Gresham.
Rescue index:	The trail is in the Portland metropolitan area.
Land status:	The City of Portland owns the trail.
Maps:	The Springwater Corridor guide is available from the Portland Parks and Recreation Bureau. Most maps of the city still display the corridor as a railroad. USGS: Damascus.

Sources of additional information: Portland Parks and Recreation Bureau (see Appendix).

Finding the trail: From Interstate 205 in Portland, take U.S. Highway 26 (Powell Boulevard) east to Gresham. Hogan Road intersects Powell Boulevard east of downtown Gresham; there is a paved parking area with restrooms at the intersection. The trailhead in Boring is not developed, but it is easy to find. In Boring, the rail line crosses Wally Road and Oregon 212. Look for the old ticket office.

THE RIDE

The route is easy to follow. The gravel sections are a little harder to ride than the paved areas, but they are well maintained.

The trail to Boring on the Springwater corridor.

The Columbia Brick Works has been in operation since 1906.

Powell Butte Park

The cinder cone volcano of Powell Butte rises 300 feet above Southeast Portland and provides exceptional views of the city and the Cascades from its peak. Douglas-fir forests surround the broad grassy summit of the butte on three sides. The 570-acre park is large enough to harbor deer and coyotes. The park has 4.3 miles of trails that are open to bicycling and the butte offers convenient singletrack climbs from the surrounding neighborhoods. The butte gives riders on the Springwater Corridor the option of getting an aerobic workout and singletrack challenges they won't find on the former rail line. The park is accessible from the Springwater Corridor, about 0.5 mile east of 136th Avenue. The Mountain View, Meadowland, and Orchard Loop trails are challenging, but they're also suitable for a beginner when the trails are dry. These same trails require intermediate riding skills when wet. Old Holgate and Pioneer Orchard trails require intermediate riding skills, regardless of weather.

General location:	Southeast Portland metro area.
Distance:	5.7 miles, as a rough figure-8.
Time:	1 hour.
Aerobic level:	Strenuous if you start from any of the three entrances at the base of the butte. Easy if you start riding from the main parking area.
Elevation change:	From the base to the summit, riders gain about 300 feet in elevation. The summit loops have about 300 feet of elevation gain.
Tread:	Mountain View Trail, 0.6 mile, is paved. The other trails are singletracks with gravel, hardpack, and cobble surfaces.
Technical difficulty:	3.
Hazards:	Watch for other park users. Many of the trail signs are missing, but try to stay on the bike trails. Riding becomes more hazardous when the trails are wet and slippery.
Season:	The park is open all year and is rarely snow-covered.
Services:	All services are available in the surrounding metropolitan area.
Rescue index:	Powell Butte is within the city of Portland.
Land status:	Portland Parks and Recreation Bureau.
Maps:	Trail maps are available at the main parking lot. USGS: Camas.

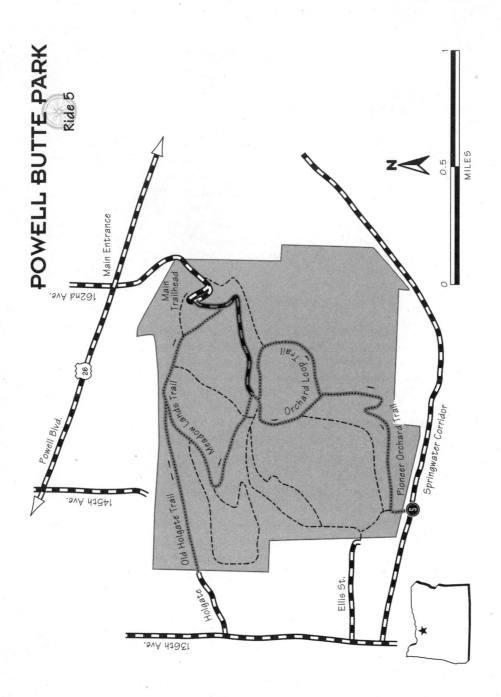

POWELL BUTTE PARK
Ride 5

Main Entrance

162nd Ave.

26

Powell Blvd.

145th Ave.

Main Trailhead

Meadow Lands Trail

Orchard Loop Trail

Old Holgate Trail

Holgate

136th Ave.

Ellis St.

Pioneer Orchard Trail

Springwater Corridor

N

0   0.5   1

MILES

Sources of additional information:
Portland Parks and Recreation Bureau
(see Appendix).

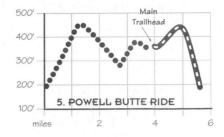

Finding the trail: From Interstate 205
in Portland, take Powell Boulevard east
to 122nd Avenue. Go right (south) on
122nd Ave. to Holgate St., and go left
on Holgate to get to the park. The park
is also accessible from the south via the
Springwater Corridor (see Ride 3), and from the main entrance at 162nd
Avenue and Powell Boulevard.

THE RIDE

First of all, please note on the park map that some trails are designated for
hikers only. Help preserve mountain bikers' access to this park by riding
only on bike trails.

From the Springwater Corridor, the Pioneer Orchard Trail climbs steadily
for 0.7 mile to its junction with the Orchard Loop Trail. Follow the Orchard Loop Trail to the right for 0.6 mile, passing the inlaid Mountain
Finder, at the crest of the hill that identifies the Cascade peaks. Turn right
on the paved Mountain View Trail and continue down the paved trail for
0.1 mile to the junction with the Meadowland Trail. Take a hard left turn

View from the top of Powell Butte.

The Old Holgate Road.

onto the Meadowland Trail and follow it clockwise to the junction with the Old Holgate Trail. The Old Holgate Trail descends on an old, cobble-covered road for 0.7 mile to the park boundary. Retrace your route back up the trail and complete the Meadowland Trail Loop to the main parking lot. Get back on the paved Mountain View Trail and follow it to its junction with the Orchard Loop Trail. Turn right, onto the Pioneer Orchard Trail, and descend to the end of the loop at the Springwater Corridor.

Forest Park: Springville Road Loop

This is only one of the many loops and rides available in Forest Park. Forest Park is the most popular place for mountain biking in Portland because of its easy access and miles of interesting and challenging trails. The trails listed below are open to bikes as of October 1997; their lengths are as follows:

Leif Erikson Drive:	11.2 miles
Holman Lane (uphill only):	0.8 mile
Firelane 1 (Yeon to 53rd St.):	2.2 miles
Firelane 3:	1 mile
Saltzman Road:	2.9 miles
Springville Road:	1 mile
Firelane 10:	1.4 miles
Newton Street:	1.9 miles
BPA Road:	2 miles
Firelane 15:	1.3 miles
Firelane 12:	1.5 miles

Obey the trail signs. The city may open new trails or close these trails, depending on user conflicts and damage. Follow IMBA rules and stay off muddy singletracks. Forest Park is on a northeast-facing slope above the Willamette River and an industrial area. The forest is dominated by Douglas-fir and big leaf maple and provides habitat for more than 100 species of birds. It offers occasional views of Mt. Saint Helens and other volcanoes.

FOREST PARK OVERVIEW MAP

Ride 6

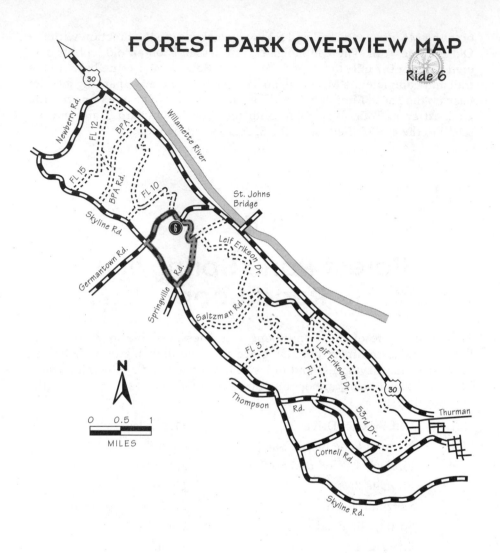

- 30
- Newberry Rd.
- FL 12
- BPA
- FL 15
- BPA Rd.
- FL 10
- Willamette River
- St. Johns Bridge
- Skyline Rd.
- 6
- Leif Erikson Dr.
- Germantown Rd.
- Springville Rd.
- Saltzman Rd.
- FL 3
- Leif Erikson Dr.
- FL 1
- 30
- N
- 0   0.5   1
- MILES
- Thompson   Rd.
- 53rd Dr.
- Thurman
- Cornell Rd.
- Skyline Rd.

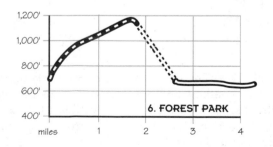

1,200'
1,000'
800'
600'
400'

miles   1   2   3   4

6. FOREST PARK

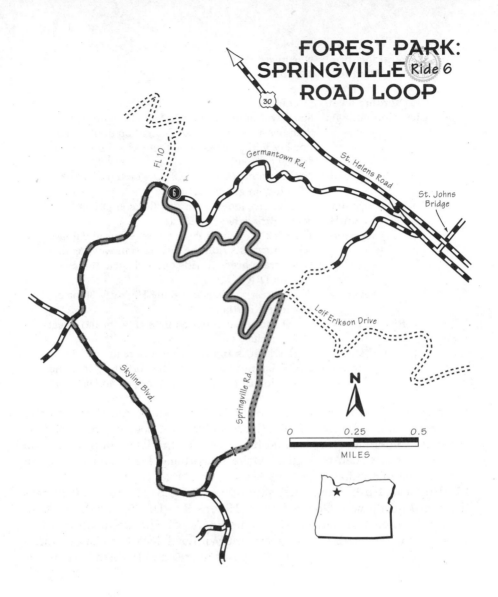

FOREST PARK: SPRINGVILLE ROAD LOOP

Ride 6

30

FL 10

6

Germantown Rd.

St. Helens Road

St. Johns Bridge

Leif Erikson Drive

Skyline Blvd.

Springville Rd.

N

| 0 | 0.25 | 0.5 |

MILES

★

General location:	Northwest Portland.
Distance:	4.3 mile loop.
Time:	1 hour.
Aerobic level:	Strenuous.
Elevation change:	Starts with a moderate 400-foot climb on paved road, then has a steep 450-foot descent on doubletrack, and finishes with a gradual 50-foot elevation gain on gravel/dirt road.
Tread:	2 miles on paved road, 0.8 mile on doubletrack, 1.5 miles on gravel/dirt road.
Technical difficulty:	3 on the fire lanes; 2 on Leif Erikson Drive.
Hazards:	Forest Park is heavily used.
Season:	The park is open all year, but severe trail damage will occur if cyclists ride the dirt trails in wet weather. When trails are wet, ride out and back on Leif Erikson Drive.
Services:	The nearest services are along Highway 30 or in Northwest Portland.
Rescue index:	Forest Park is surrounded by highways and streets and is in the city.
Land status:	Portland Parks and Recreation Bureau.
Maps:	USGS: Linnton; Portland. The Portland Parks and Recreation Bureau also publishes an adequate map.

Sources of additional information: *One City's Wilderness, Portland's Forest Park* by Marcy Cottrell Houle (Oregon Historical Society Press, 1996) is the most comprehensive guide to the park. For the latest information on which trails are open to cyclists, write to Portland Parks and Recreation Bureau (see Appendix).

Finding the trail: From Interstate 405, take U.S. Highway 30 Bypass (Lombard Road) west. Go west on St. Helens Rd. (US 30) and drive about 0.25 mile, then turn left on Germantown Road. The trailhead is about 1 mile uphill. When driving up Germantown Road, look for a large natural bowl on the left side of the road; the parking area and trailhead are in this bowl.

THE RIDE

Start the ride with a climb up Germantown Road to Skyline Boulevard. Turn left on Skyline and continue climbing for about 1 mile before taking another left onto Springville Road. If you come to Springville Road, on the right, you are 0.25 mile past the left turn. Follow Springville Road past a locked gate and veer to the left at the junction with Firelane 7 to stay on Springville Road. Turn left when you get to Leif Erikson Drive for a short trip back to the trailhead.

Springville Road in Forest Park.

Oregon's Coast and Coast Range

Oregon's first rail-to-trail state park leads into the Coast Range from the edge of the Portland metropolitan area. The 22-mile trail winds through the hills between the towns of Banks and Vernonia. It has enough elevation gain and distance to tire out most cyclists, and it is open year-round. It does not get much use and would be a pleasant outing for a family.

Oregon's coastline is spectacular with its jutting headlands, coves, and beaches. Unfortunately, the Bayocean Peninsula is one of only a few non-motorized routes for bicyclists on the coast. It is a leisurely ride along Tillamook Bay and ends at the jetty. More adventurous cyclists head into the Coast Range to explore.

Large portions of the Coast Range are owned by private timber companies and many of these companies have closed their roads to motorized vehicles. Bicycling and hiking are usually still allowed, but you should check before you enter private land. Sometimes the gates will have signs that say non-motorized use is allowed. Some companies will even provide maps of their property, upon request.

The Tillamook State Forest is the largest block of public land in the northern Coast Range. The Tillamook's managers have designated sections of the forest for non-motorized recreation; these rarely used roads develop a soft surface of needles and leaves that makes for smooth cycling. Two of the Tillamook's few singletracks are described below, but don't limit your explorations to singletracks. The roads are open all year and they offer challenging climbs, screaming descents, and stream-side solitude. Get a map before you go (see Maps, below), because it is easy to get confused if you travel very far.

Farther south along the coast, the Siuslaw National Forest covers nearly 700,000 acres. It too has closed many roads to motorized vehicles, but bicyclists are welcome. The Siuslaw has also been reclaiming many roads, so Ranger District maps may not be accurate. The Mary's Peak Recreation Area contains the most extensive system of singletrack on the coast that is open to bikes. Meadows cover the summit of Mary's Peak, allowing 360-degree views. Nearby, McDonald Experimental Forest attracts cyclists from Oregon State University in Corvallis. The University has constructed several loop rides in the forest by connecting roads with short trails. The roads are closed to motorized vehicles, which makes for better cycling.

Banks/Vernonia State Park

This is Oregon's first rail-to-trail state park and connects the towns of Banks and Vernonia. The trail follows the West Fork of Dairy Creek through farmland and pastures before climbing into the Coast Range through stands of Douglas-fir, alder, and hemlock, followed by a descent into the Nehalem River Valley and Vernonia. The Banks to Vernonia rail line was built in the 1920s and hauled billions of board feet of lumber from the Oregon-American Lumber Mill, in Vernonia, to Portland. You can still see the stumps of trees that were 4 to 8 feet in diameter from the trail. There are two trestles in the park (Buxton and Tophill), 80 feet high and 600 feet long, that are visible from the trail. This is a good trail to ride in winter, when most trails are too muddy or snow-covered. Logging is still the main industry in Vernonia, and the surrounding hills are some of the most productive timber-growing lands in the world. In summer, the town creates a swimming hole in the Nehalem River with a rope swing over the water. This is a refreshing stop on a hot summer day. You can't miss the park near the center of this small town. While the grades on this trail rarely exceed 3 percent, the continual climbing to reach Tophill Pass can be strenuous.

General location:	18 miles northwest of Portland.
Distance:	41 miles, out and back.
Time:	5 to 6 hours.
Aerobic level:	Strenuous, if you complete the entire trail out and back.
Elevation change:	From Banks, the trail gradually climbs 750 feet to a pass at Tophill and then descends 300 feet to Vernonia. Only when the trail circumvents the two trestles does it have grades in excess of 3 percent.
Tread:	Converted rail line. Nearly half the trail is paved, including a continuous 7-mile segment near Vernonia. The rest is gravel in good to excellent condition.
Technical difficulty:	Primarily 1, some short sections of 3.
Hazards:	On rare occasions, snow may make the trail impassable. Frost is a more common problem and it may make the paved sections very slippery. Watch for equestrians and announce your presence.
Season:	The trail is rideable year-round.
Services:	Most services are available in Banks and Vernonia.
Rescue index:	The Park Manager's office is near the Buxton Trailhead. Help is also available in Vernonia.

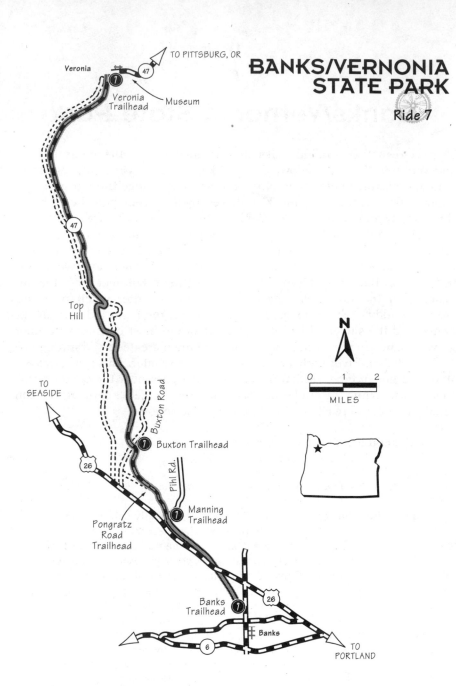

BANKS/VERNONIA STATE PARK
Ride 7

Veronia

TO PITTSBURG, OR

47

Veronia Trailhead

Museum

47

Top Hill

Buxton Road

TO SEASIDE

Buxton Trailhead

26

Pihl Rd.

Manning Trailhead

Pongratz Road Trailhead

N

0   1   2
MILES

Banks Trailhead

26

Banks

6

TO PORTLAND

The Buxton railroad trestle on the Banks/Vernonia Trail.

Land status: Vernonia State Park. (This is a very narrow park; stay on the trail or you will be trespassing.)
Maps: A park map is available by writing the Oregon Parks and Recreation Division (see Appendix). USGS: Meacham Corner, Buxton, Vernonia.

Sources of additional information: When you're in Vernonia, visit the museum on Oregon 47, east of downtown. The museum has a large number of old photographs of the Oregon-American lumber mill, as well as logging displays.

Finding the trail: From Interstate 5 in Portland, take U.S. Highway 26 west about 27 miles to where it intersects with Oregon 47. The Banks Trailhead is located north of Banks on OR 47. The trailhead in Vernonia is at Anderson Park.

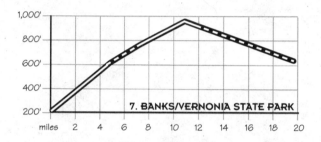

THE RIDE

The first 4 miles from Banks to Manning parallel OR 47 and US 26. At Manning, riders must leave the trail and ride on Pongratz Road for 1 mile before getting back on the railroad grade. Pongratz Road is narrow and without a shoulder, so use caution. You may want to start at Pongratz Trailhead or Buxton Trailhead to avoid riding on Pongratz Road.

The trail around the Tophill Trestle has a short but steep descent on loose rock and mud. Walking is advised for this short section. The 1996 floods washed-out several culverts along the trail. The trail has been routed around these slides, but the slopes near the slides are still unstable—stay back from the edge. These slides are examples of the damage roads can cause to rivers and salmon habitat. You can see how thousands of cubic yards of mud and debris were washed into streams when the culverts washed out.

Gales Creek

From the cottonwoods and alders along Gales Creek, the trail climbs 632 feet through young Douglas-fir to its junction with Oregon Highway 6, the Wilson River Highway. The trail follows a railroad grade for a short distance. If your breathing is not too loud, you will hear the long melodic song of the winter wren, a small gray bird. The long, slow climb, with your head down and heart pounding, will give you a chance to watch for deer, elk, and bear tracks on the trail. The ride down the trail is exciting enough to make you forget how hard it was to climb to the highway. The 240-thousand–acre Tillamook Burn started in logging slash, about 0.5 mile north of Gales Creek Campground in August 1933. The Tillamook State Forest encourages non-motorized use north of Highway 6 and allows ATV use south of the highway. When the trails are too wet to ride, try the roads north of the highway.

General location:	41 miles west of Portland on the Wilson River Highway (OR 6).
Distance:	4.2 miles, out and back.
Time:	1 hour.
Aerobic level:	Strenuous.
Elevation change:	632 feet of elevation gain and loss.
Tread:	Well-maintained, dirt singletrack.
Technical difficulty:	3, some sections of 4.
Hazards:	By starting your ride at Gales Creek, you become aware of most hazards on your way up. Downfalls and washouts may be encountered. Do not ride the trail if it is wet.
Season:	Dry-weather riding. A little rain makes this trail too slippery to climb or descend.
Services:	Banks, 15 miles east of Gales Creek Campground, has most services.
Rescue index:	Seek help in Portland, 41 miles east, or Banks, 15 miles east.
Land status:	Tillamook State Forest.
Maps:	To obtain recreation maps, call the Oregon State Department of Forestry office (see Appendix). USGS: Timber.

Sources of additional information: Oregon State Department of Forestry (see Appendix).

Finding the trail: Gales Creek Campground and Trailhead are 41 miles west of Portland, off of OR 6. The Rogers Road turnoff to Gale Creek Campground is on the north side of the highway, about 1 mile after entering the

GALES CREEK
Ride 8

NELS ROGERS–
UNIVERSITY FALLS
Ride 9

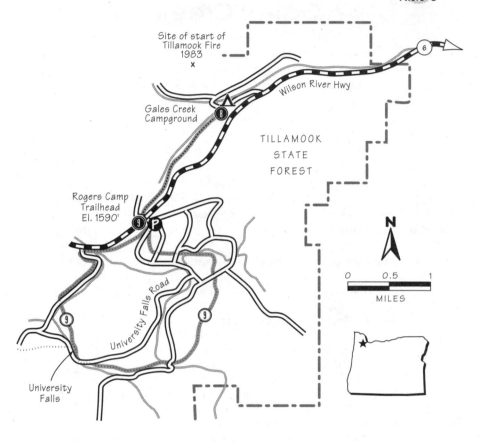

Site of start of
Tillamook Fire
1983
x

Gales Creek
Campground

Wilson River Hwy

TILLAMOOK
STATE
FOREST

Rogers Camp
Trailhead
El. 1590'

University Falls Road

University
Falls

N

0   0.5   1
MILES

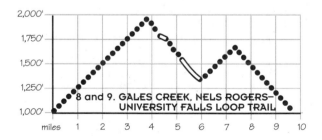

8 and 9. GALES CREEK, NELS ROGERS–
UNIVERSITY FALLS LOOP TRAIL

miles   1   2   3   4   5   6   7   8   9   10

Tillamook State Forest. Follow the signs to Gales Creek Campground. The trailhead is near the restrooms.

THE RIDE

A short, gravel interpretive trail leads to the left near the trailhead and provides a short warm-up loop. The trail crosses several wooden bridges that are usually slippery. The top and bottom portions of the trail follow a railroad grade, and part of an old trestle is still visible near the top of the trail. This trail can be combined with the Nels Rogers–University Falls Loop Trail for a longer, more challenging ride.

See Map on Page 42

Nels Rogers–University Falls Loop Trail

The trailhead at Rogers Camp is the trailhead for an extensive ATV trail system. It was the site of the 1949 ceremony that began reforestation after the Tillamook Burn. Large, charred stumps are visible from the trail. The trail winds through Douglas-fir forests, clearcuts, and thinnings. It crosses several ATV trails, roads, and streams before reaching University Falls. University Falls is a thunderous torrent in winter, but it is only a cool shower in late summer. A portion of the trail follows an elk migration route. The uneven tread and numerous roots make for a challenging ride.

General location:	43 miles west of Portland.
Distance:	7.5 miles, loop.
Time:	1 hour.
Aerobic level:	Moderate.
Elevation change:	From Rogers Camp, the trail climbs 300 feet to Saddle Mountain Road, descends 500 feet to University Falls and Elliott Creek, then climbs 200 feet to reach the trailhead.
Tread:	Dirt singletrack for 6.5 miles, gravel road for 1 mile.
Technical difficulty:	3, some sections of 4.
Hazards:	Watch and listen for ATVs at trail and road crossings. Portions of the trail may be slippery, even in dry weather. Heavy trail use has exposed roots.
Season:	This is a dry-season trail, do not try to ride it in winter or after heavy rain.

Overgrown logging roads in the Coast Range offer excellent mountain biking.

Services:	Banks, 17 miles east, has most services.
Rescue index:	Help is available in Portland or Banks.
Land status:	Tillamook State Forest.
Maps:	To obtain recreation maps, call the Oregon State Department of Forestry office (see Appendix A). USGS: Timber.

Sources of additional information: Oregon State Department of Forestry (see Appendix A).

Finding the trail: From Portland, take U.S. Highway 26 northwest to Oregon 6. Go west on OR 6 until you enter the Tillamook State Forest; Rogers Camp is about 4 miles past the entrance. A large pullout is on the north side of the highway just before the turn to Rogers Camp, which is on the south side of the highway. The trail starts about 50 yards up a fire road, near the entrance to the Rogers Camp parking lot.

THE RIDE

Watch for ATVs descending the fire road at the trailhead. A sign identifies the non-motorized singletrack. The trail begins with a moderate climb around a hill. In its first 3 miles, the trail crosses several ATV trails, roads, a powerline, and streams at right angles, so it is easy to keep on the trail. The second half of the trail runs on and off gravel roads, but the exits from the roads, back onto the trail, are signed and easy to find.

The second half of this loop is called the Gravelle Brothers Trail on state forest maps. The trail intersects with OR 6 after running along a gravel road for almost 1 mile. It then drops below the highway, after crossing a culvert, and follows the highway on the south side until it reaches a road leading to the Department of Transportation gravel stockpiles. The trail goes around the back of the stockpiles, away from the highway, and back to Rogers Camp.

Bayocean Peninsula

This easy route on Bayocean Peninsula along Tillamook Bay is a perfect location to picnic after stopping at the Blue Heron and Tillamook cheese factories for supplies. Picnic tables tucked in thickets of shorepine and salal near the north end of the peninsula offer protection from the wind.

The Bayocean road provided access to the former community of Bayocean and for construction of the jetty. Pacific storms have washed away almost all traces of the community.

This ride is a good one to do with children who ride proficiently. It is one of the few coastline rides in Oregon where motorized vehicles are prohibited. The road, which runs along the bay side of the peninsula, offers views of the Coast Range, dairies, and Tillamook Bay. The Pacific Ocean is a few

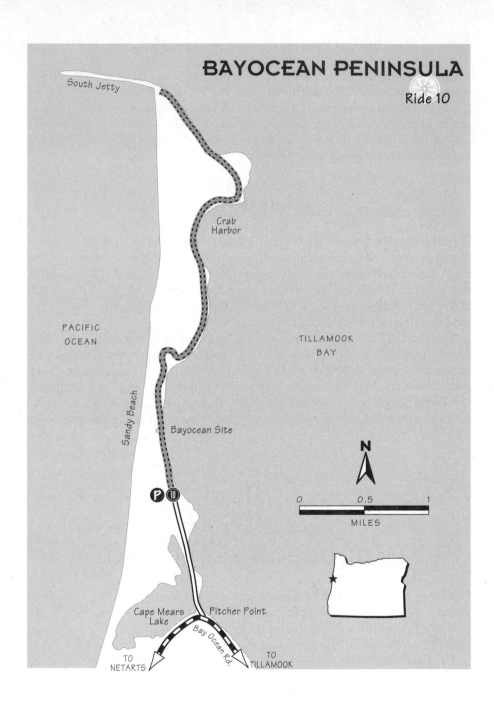

BAYOCEAN PENINSULA

Ride 10

South Jetty

Crab
Harbor

PACIFIC
OCEAN

TILLAMOOK
BAY

Sandy Beach

Bayocean Site

N

0   0.5   1
MILES

P 10

Cape Mears
Lake

Pitcher Point

Bay Ocean Rd.

TO
NETARTS

TO
TILLAMOOK

hundred yards across the beach, from the north end of the road. You can almost always see seals and sea lions near the jetty. When salmon are running, the bay will be crowded with boats. Birders find dozens of species in the varied habitats along the road, and low tides bring in hundreds of shorebirds.

General location:	The trail starts at Bayocean parking lot, which is 7 miles northwest of Tillamook in northwest Oregon.
Distance:	7.2 miles, out and back.
Time:	1 hour.
Aerobic level:	Easy.
Elevation change:	Flat for its entire length.
Tread:	Gravel road with sandy sections, closed to motorized vehicles.
Technical difficulty:	2.
Hazards:	The trail is popular, so watch for other users.
Season:	The trail is open year-round.
Services:	All services are available in Tillamook. The parking lot has toilets, but no water.
Rescue index:	Help can be found in Tillamook.
Land status:	The peninsula is a Tillamook County park.
Maps:	The visitor information center at the Tillamook Cheese factory north of Tillamook provides free maps of the area. USGS: Garibaldi.

Sources of additional information: Tillamook County Parks Department (see Appendix).

Finding the trail: From downtown Tillamook, take the Netarts Highway (3rd Street) west. After crossing the Tillamook River, 2 miles west of Tillamook, turn right on Bayocean Road. The turnoff to the Bayocean parking lot is 5 miles north of the Bayocean Road–Netarts Highway intersection.

THE RIDE

The ride from the north end of the parking lot passes through beach grass, sand dunes, salal thickets, and forest before reaching the jetty. The last few hundred yards to the jetty may be covered with soft sand. You can add a couple miles to this ride by starting at the Pitcher Point pullout. Pitcher Point has an interpretive sign that summarizes the history of Bayocean. The ride to the Bayocean parking lot provides views of Cape Meares Lake.

Mary's Peak

At 4,097 feet, Mary's Peak is the highest point in Oregon's Coast Range. On clear days, the peak offers views of the Cascades, the Coast Range, and the Willamette Valley, but clear days are rare here. On a more typical day, you will be buffeted by wind and rain on the open slopes around the summit. Breaks in the heavy masses of clouds allow views of the meadows and surrounding forests. You get the feeling of being on top of the world as you look down on the next wall of clouds being blown in from the ocean. The communication facilities on the summit provide some shelter from the wind and, if it is not too stormy, this is an inspiring place for a picnic. The blue green tops of noble firs are easy to distinguish from the darker green of the Douglas-firs in the surrounding forests. The alpine meadows host a variety of wildlife, including coyotes and elk.

The area offers more than 10 miles of singletrack, with several loop options for experienced bicyclists. The physically demanding trails provide a technical challenge for intermediate and advanced riders. Start at the Woods Creek Trailhead for an exhausting elevation gain of more than 2,300 feet. Try Forest Road 2005 if you are looking for an easier ride that is sheltered from storms. The gravel road to the summit is too steep for novice riders. The Forest Service charges a fee to park at Mary's Peak.

Heading down from Mary's Peak.

MARY'S PEAK
Ride 11

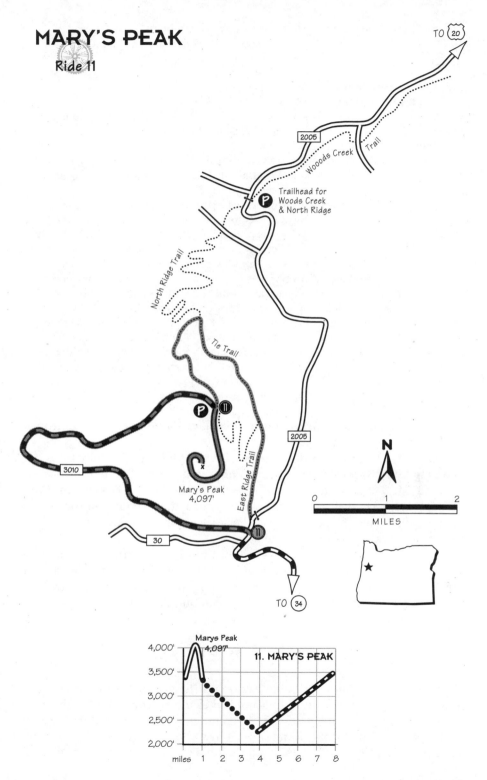

TO 20

2005

Wooods Creek Trail

Trailhead for
Woods Creek
& North Ridge

North Ridge Trail

Tie Trail

P

11

2005

3010

x

Mary's Peak
4,097'

East Ridge Trail

30

TO 34

N

0   1   2
MILES

Marys Peak
4,097'

11. MARY'S PEAK

4,000'

3,500'

3,000'

2,500'

2,000'

miles   1   2   3   4   5   6   7   8

General location:	Mary's Peak observation point parking area is 25 miles southwest of downtown Corvallis.
Distance:	7.8 miles, loop.
Time:	1 to 2 hours.
Aerobic level:	Strenuous.
Elevation change:	1,800 feet.
Tread:	Singletrack for 2.8 miles, gravel road for 1.2 miles, and paved road for 3.8 miles.
Technical difficulty:	4.
Hazards:	The trails are steep and especially treacherous when wet. Windfalls are common. Control your speed on all descents.
Season:	It rarely snows in the Coast Range, but the singletracks may be impassable during wet weather. The trails drain quickly and may be ridden after two or three days without rain. Wildflowers bloom in the meadows and forests from April through July.
Services:	All services are available in Corvallis. Gas, food, and phones, are available in Philomath and Alsea.
Rescue index:	Help is available in Philomath and Alsea.
Land status:	Siuslaw National Forest, Waldport Ranger District.
Maps:	A pamphlet entitled "Marys Peak—A Place to Discover" is available from the Siuslaw National Forest. It is the best source of information about the area. The USGS Quad for Mary's Peak and the Alsea Ranger District map do not show bike trails.

Sources of additional information: Siuslaw National Forest (see Appendix A).

Finding the trail: From downtown Corvallis, take U.S. Highway 20/Oregon Highway 34 west for 6 miles to Philomath. From Philomath, continue west on OR 34 for 10 miles and turn right on the Mary's Peak Road. Don't forget to get your day-use permit at the information station on the Mary's Peak Road. Follow the paved Mary's Peak Road for 9.3 miles to the observation point parking area below the summit.

You can reach the Woods Creek Trailhead by going north from Philomath on U.S. Highway 20 for about 1.8 miles and turning left onto Forest Road 2005/Benton County Road 26440. Follow this road for 7.5 miles to the gate across Forest Road 2005 and park in the pullout. Do not block the road.

THE RIDE

From the observation parking area, ride up the gravel road to the summit and back down. The North Ridge Trail leaves the northeast end of the parking lot. Follow the trail for 0.6 mile to its junction with the Tie Trail, on the right. The junction is easy to miss. Look for a log bench near the junction. Follow the Tie Trail for 1.1 miles to its junction with the East Ridge Trail.

The Tie Trail crosses a couple of precipitous headwalls that may scare you into dismounting. Continue the descent on the East Ridge Trail to the gate on Forest Road 2005. The Marys Peak Road is just past the gate. You can return to the observation point trailhead on the paved road (3.8 miles), backtrack on the Tie Trail (2.8 miles), or loop back on the East Ridge Trail (2.5 miles). If the trails are damp, they may not offer enough traction to ride uphill.

Other trails: The North Ridge Trail from the observation parking lot to the trailhead on Forest Road 2005 is 3.8 miles. From this trailhead you can ride 2.0 miles east, parallel to FR 2005 on the Woods Creek Trail. The distance from lower gate to the upper gate on FR 2005 is 3.4 miles.

McDonald Forest: Calloway Creek to Cap House Loop

McDonald Forest covers 7,000 acres in the Coast Range and has more than 60 miles of roads and trails to explore. Ride the Intensive Management Trail to see how the distance between trees in a stand influences their diameter—the closer to each other the trees are, the smaller their diameter. Another practice being studied by Oregon State University in McDonald Forest is the pruning of trees' lower boles to produce high-grade lumber for furniture and other specialty products. The thinned and pruned stands are surprisingly pleasing to the eye compared to the dense, unmanaged thickets of Douglas-fir. The forestry department at Oregon State University has been studying the forest for more than 70 years with an eye toward sustainability and improved timber harvests. The forest has a few small stands of old growth, but bikes are not allowed on the trails that access these stands. Clearcuts near the ridgetop offer views of farmed valleys, the Coast Range, and the Cascades.

The route described below includes a vigorous climb and several miles of singletrack. For a longer ride, head up Road 500 and follow it along the ridgeline to Sulfur Springs Road, then loop back on Road 580.

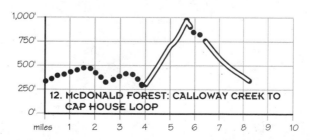

12. McDONALD FOREST: CALLOWAY CREEK TO CAP HOUSE LOOP

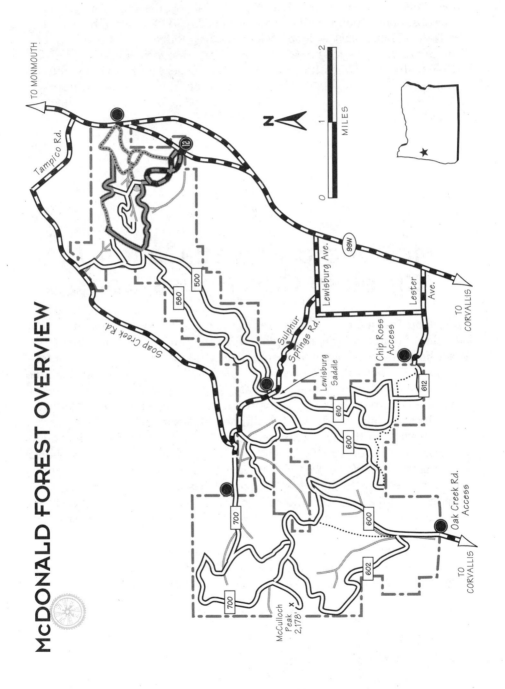

McDONALD FOREST OVERVIEW

TO MONMOUTH

Tampico Rd.

Soap Creek Rd.

99W

Lewisburg Ave.

Lester Ave.

TO CORVALLIS

Chip Ross Access

612

610

600

602

Lewisburg Saddle

Sulphur Springs Rd.

500

580

700

700

600

McCulloch Peak x 2,178'

Oak Creek Rd. Access

TO CORVALLIS

N

MILES

0   1   2

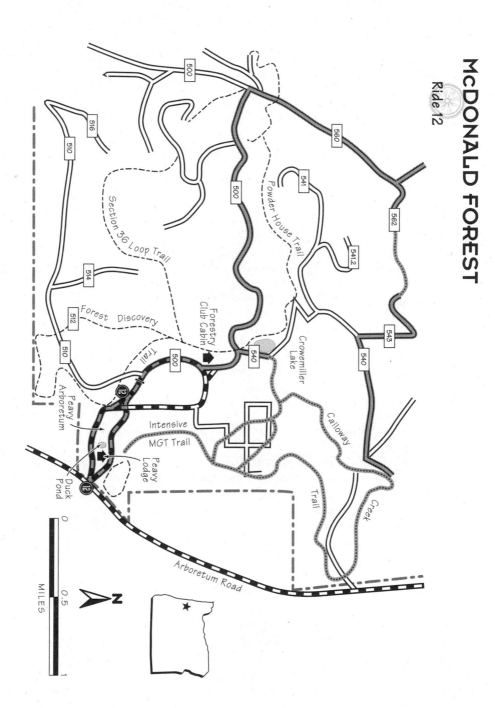

McDONALD FOREST
Ride 12

Section 36 Loop Trail

Forest Discovery

Trail

Forestry Club Cabin

Powder House Trail

Peavy Arboretum

Intensive MGT Trail

Peavy Lodge

Duck Pond

Crowemiller Lake

Calloway

Creek

Trail

Arboretum Road

500

516

510

514

512

510

500

541

560

562

541.2

543

540

540

MILES

0   0.5   1

N

General location:	The main entrance to McDonald Forest is 6 miles north of Corvallis, off of U.S. Highway 99W.
Distance:	8.4 miles, three loops.
Time:	1 to 2 hours.
Aerobic level:	Moderate.
Elevation change:	The trail, most of which is on Road 500, climbs about 650 feet.
Tread:	The route is a hardpacked dirt singletrack for 3.9 miles and gravel road for 4.5 miles.
Technical difficulty:	Level 3.
Hazards:	The trail connecting roads 562 and 543 is very steep. Anticipate other recreationists, including equestrians. Announce your presence well in advance of overtaking other users and be prepared to yield the right of way.
Season:	You can ride most of the roads year-round, but some may be closed for management activities. The trails should be used only from May to October.
Services:	All services are available in Corvallis.
Rescue index:	Help is available in Corvallis, but the forest office may be contacted in emergencies.
Land status:	Oregon State University Research Forest.
Maps:	The bike shops in Corvallis sell an excellent map of the forest. The McDonald Research Forest Visitor Map and Guide is usually available at the trailheads. USGS 7.5 minute quads for Corvallis and Airlie South cover the area, but they are not good sources of road and trail information.

Sources of additional information: McDonald Research Forest (see Appendix).

Finding the trail: Take U.S. Highway 99W north from Corvallis for 6 miles, then turn left on Arboretum Road. Follow the Arboretum Road for about 0.5 mile to the Arboretum entrance. Keep to the right after you enter the Arboretum, passing a parking lot on the right and Peavy Lodge on the left. Park at the second parking lot to access the Intensive Management Trail. Brochures should be available at the trailhead.

THE RIDE

Follow the Intensive Management Trail through demonstrations of thinning and pruning. Stop and read the interpretive signs if this is your first visit. When you pass the start of the Calloway Creek Trail, you have two options: hop on it immediately, or complete the loop of the Intensive Management Trail. Follow the Calloway Creek Trail as it dips and climbs through forests and clearcuts, until it ends on Road 540 at Cronemiller Lake. Head south (left) on Road 540 for 0.25 mile to its junction with Road 500. Turn uphill (right) on Road 500 and climb to the top where it meets Road 560. Road 560 passes the powder house and Powder House Trail after less than 0.25 mile. Stay on Road 560 until it reaches a fork with Road 562. Turn right onto Road 562. The road soon becomes a steep, rutted trail along a clearcut. Rational riders will walk this steep trail, which ends on Road 543 after 400 yards. Follow Road 543 to Road 540. If you turn left on Road 540 you can get back on the Calloway and Intensive Management trails and follow them back to the trailhead. Turn right on Road 540 to get back to Cronemiller Lake and Road 500. Turn left on Road 500 and pass the Forestry Club Cabin and an interpretive display at the end of the road. Take a right on the paved road for a quick loop, or look at some of the two hundred species of trees and shrubs in Peavy Arboretum.

Columbia River Gorge

The Columbia River Gorge is one of the most spectacular landscapes in the Pacific Northwest. Dozens of waterfalls spill over the basalt cliffs along the Gorge; Multnomah Falls, with a drop of 620 feet, is the tallest. Interstate 84 gives Portlanders quick access to the recreational opportunites in this National Scenic Area, but most pass by the Sandy River Delta on their way to more dramatic scenery.

The Sandy River Delta (Ride 16) has miles of trails that are open to mountain bikes, and their sandy surfaces are rideable year-round. Most of the trails in the Gorge are either closed to bicycles or are too steep to ride, but some of the forest roads are worth exploring. The Tanner Creek Road (Ride 13) is one of these side roads.

The Historic Columbia River Highway, between Crown Point and Dodson, is one of the most beautiful stretches of highway in America. It is open to automobiles, but has relatively little traffic on weekday mornings. Two sections of the Historic Columbia River Highway have recently been restored and are closed to automobiles. These sections, described in Rides 14 and 15, are great rides for families. Don't limit your explorations to the bike rides; try a sternwheeler cruise or a ride on the Mt. Hood Railroad. Visit some of the museums, hit the small towns during one of their numerous festivals, or explore some of the miles of hiking trails winding through the forest.

Tanner Creek Road

This short but strenuous climb on a forest road into Tanner Creek canyon is rarely used. However, the route is seldom blocked by ice and snow and, since it is passable when wet, it is a good place to ride year-round. The trail runs through a Douglas-fir forest; sword ferns and the clover-like oxalis carpet the forest floor. The road occasionally emerges at cliffs for views of the canyon. Originally, the road provided access for construction of the powerlines from Bonneville Dam and passes under the lines several times. Several trails emerge from or cross the road, including the Tanner Butte Trail 401, Wahclella Falls Trail, Tanner Creek Trail 431, and the Gorge Trail 400. Wahclella Falls and the hike to up Trail 401 to Wauna Point are worthwhile diversions. Only the Gorge Trail is open to bikes.

TANNER CREEK ROAD

Ride 13

EAGLE CREEK OVERLOOK TO BONNEVILLE DAM

Ride 14

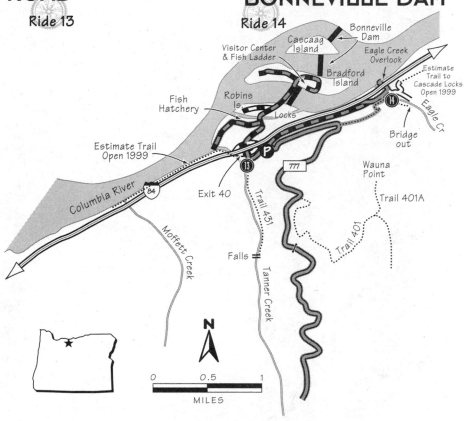

General location:	40 miles east of Portland on Interstate 84.
Distance:	12 miles, out and back.
Time:	2 hours.
Aerobic level:	Strenuous
Elevation change:	From the Wahclella Falls (also called Tanner Falls) parking area (elevation 60 feet), the route climbs 1600 feet before descending 450 feet to Tanner Creek at the far end of the route.
Tread:	Gravel road with a portion closed to motorized vehicles.
Technical difficulty:	2.
Hazards:	Moderately steep grades, slippery road, falling rocks, and cliffs require caution when riding on this road.
Season:	This is a good trail to ride any time of year, except during periods of snow and ice.
Services:	Cascade Locks has most services and is three miles east of the Bonneville Dam exit.

Found along the Tanner Creek Road, these massive powerlines transport electricity from Bonneville Dam.

Rescue index: Help may be available at the Bonneville Dam and Fish Hatchery or in Cascade Locks.

Land status: Columbia River Gorge National Scenic Area, Mt. Hood National Forest.

Maps: USGS 7.5 minute quad: Tanner Butte. The Columbia Gorge Ranger District map provides better information than the quad map, but the Mount Hood National Forest recreation map is adequate.

Sources of additional information: Columbia River Gorge National Scenic Area (see Appendix A).

Finding the trail: Take the Bonneville Dam exit (exit 40) from Interstate 84 and park at either the Wahclella Falls Trailhead, on the south side of I-84, or the large new parking area 0.5 mile east of the trailhead, overlooking I-84.

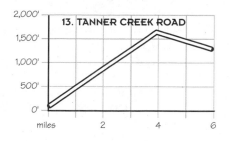

THE RIDE

From Wahclella Falls Trailhead, take the bike path east to the large parking lot. Forest Road 777 (gravel) climbs very steeply away from the parking lot on a series of switchbacks. The paved Historic Columbia River Highway heads east from the parking lot to Eagle Creek. About 1 mile from the trailhead, the road switches back and climbs to the west. Trail 400 heads east from the switchback and is an alternative route to Eagle Creek (see Ride 14). Several spur roads take off from FR 777, but the through-road is easy to recognize. Leaves and other debris on the road can make descents dangerous if you do not control your speed. After climbing steadily for 4 miles, the road emerges from the forest on top of some cliffs. The road then descends for 2 miles before ending near Tanner Creek. The ride back is surprisingly easy.

See Map on Page 57

Eagle Creek Overlook to Bonneville Dam

Families may enjoy this interesting tour, or it can be added to the Tanner Creek Road (Ride 13) as a warm-up for those wanting a more strenuous workout. Starting at the Overlook picnic area, the ride passes the Eagle Creek Fish Hatchery and uses a recently reopened section of the Historic Columbia River Highway (HCRH), which rounds Tooth Rock on its way to Bonneville Dam. It passes by the Bonneville powerhouse, visitor center, fish ladder, navigation locks, and fish hatchery, all of which are worthy of a stop. The dam is especially impressive in spring when the spillway is open.

Underwater windows let visitors watch salmon climbing the fish ladder. The route is rarely closed by snow and ice and the visitor centers are open year-round, except on major holidays. A short hike from the route at Tanner Creek leads to beautiful Wahclella Falls.

General location:	41 miles east of Portland near Interstate 84.
Distance:	7.8 miles, out and back.
Time:	1 to2 hours.
Aerobic level:	Easy.
Elevation change:	Only 200 feet of elevation change.
Tread:	Paved road, portions closed to motorized vehicles.
Technical difficulty:	1.
Hazards:	Steel grating in front of the dam, slippery roads, traffic, and falling rocks require caution, especially in wet weather.
Season:	This is a good ride at any time of year, except in snow and ice. Salmon climb the fish ladders from April through September.
Services:	Cascade Locks has most services and is 2 miles east of the Eagle Creek exit.
Rescue index:	Help may be available at the Bonneville Dam and Fish Hatchery, Eagle Creek Hatchery, or in Cascade Locks.
Land status:	Columbia River Gorge National Scenic Area, Mount Hood National Forest; Army Corps of Engineers.
Maps:	USGS 7.5 minute quads: Tanner Butte and Bonneville Dam. The Columbia Gorge Ranger District map provides better information than the quad map, but the Mount Hood National Forest recreation map is adequate.

Sources of additional information: Columbia River Gorge National Scenic Area; Bonneville Dam Visitor Center (see Appendix).
Finding the trail: Take the Eagle Creek exit (exit 41) from Interstate 84 and go under the freeway to Overlook picnic area

THE RIDE

From Overlook picnic area, ride back under the freeway and west over Eagle Creek to the new stairs leading to the Historic Columbia River Highway (HCRH). You will be riding against traffic coming off of the freeway, so use extreme caution and get off the road as soon as possible. Follow the HCRH around Tooth Rock and past the parking lot. Go under the freeway to Bonneville Dam. Loop around the fish hatchery, then up the hill passing the locks and in front of the powerhouse. Cross over the fish ladder to get to the west end of Bradford Island, then backtrack to the visitor center. Return the same way.

Alternate route 1: A more challenging return route uses Trail 400. Weather permitting, climb Forest Road 777 to access the Gorge Trail. About 1 mile from the Bonneville Dam underpass, the road switches back and climbs to the west. Trail 400 heads east from the switchback, watch for the signs. About 0.3 mile down the trail, a new trail has been constructed that drops to the left toward the Columbia River. Take the new trail. The old trail leads to the site of a washed-out suspension bridge over Eagle Creek.

Alternate route 2: In 1999, the Historic Columbia River Highway will be opened for bikes from Moffett Creek to Cascade Locks. The 7 miles between Cascade Locks and Moffett Creek have great views of the dam, river, bridges, and cliffs. The trailhead in Cascade Locks will be under the Bridge of the Gods. The trail will connect to the road at the Overlook picnic area.

To get to Moffett Creek, cross Tanner Creek on the HCRH. The HCRH is being extended under I-84 to run down the river side of the freeway to Moffett Creek. The total length of this out-and-back bike route is 14.8 miles.

Hood River to Mosier

This short section (officially opens in 1999) of the Historic Columbia River Highway (HCRH) is open to bikes and hikers at both ends. There is a shed to protect visitors from rock-falls, just west of the Mosier Twin Tunnels

Newspapers heralded the HCRH as the most beautiful road in the world when it opened in 1922. The section between Hood River and Mosier runs through pine and oak savannas with views of the Columbia River and Cascade peaks. Basalt cliffs line the road and provide perches for raptors. A detour to Panorama Point Park is highly recommended, especially in April and May when the orchards are blooming.

Hood River is a sailboarder's mecca, and they come from around the world to catch the winds funneled through the Columbia Gorge. When the winds aren't blowing, many windsurfers head to the hills to mountain bike. Hood River has dozens of singletracks within an hour's drive that are open to bikes. Sporting goods stores, cafes, and other shops keep the downtown bustling.

General location:	Hood River and Mosier in northwest Oregon.
Distance:	12.2 miles, out and back from Hood River.
Time:	1 to 2 hours.
Aerobic level:	Easy.
Elevation change:	Gradual 300-foot climb and descent on the HCRH. Add another 300 feet of elevation gain if you go to Panorama Point.

Biking on the Historic Columbia River Highway, dubbed the "most beautiful road in the world" when it opened in 1922.

Tread:	Paved road, closed to motorized vehicles.
Technical difficulty:	1.
Hazards:	Falling rocks are a hazard near cliffs.
Season:	Open year-round, except during severe winter weather.
Services:	All services are available in Hood River. Mosier has most services.
Rescue index:	Help is available in Hood River.
Land status:	Oregon State Park and county roads.
Maps:	Portions of the road are visible on the 7.5 minute USGS quad for White Salmon.

Sources of additional information: Most local bike shops carry *The Singletrack Anthology: Hood River.* This publication describes 18 rides in the Hood River area. For information on this trail contact Oregon State Parks (see Appendix A.)

Finding the trail: To access the tunnels, take the Mosier exit off of Interstate 84. After crossing the railroad tracks, loop back under the off-ramp by taking two hard left turns onto Rock Creek Road. Follow Rock Creek Road for 0.8 mile to the new parking lot for the Historic Columbia River Highway on the left side of the road. The entrance to the HCRH trail is 100 yards back down Rock Creek Road and climbs to the west.

From downtown Hood River, head east on State Street (U.S.Highway 30) and cross Hood River. Cross Oregon Highway 35 to get on the Old Columbia River Road (the HCRH).

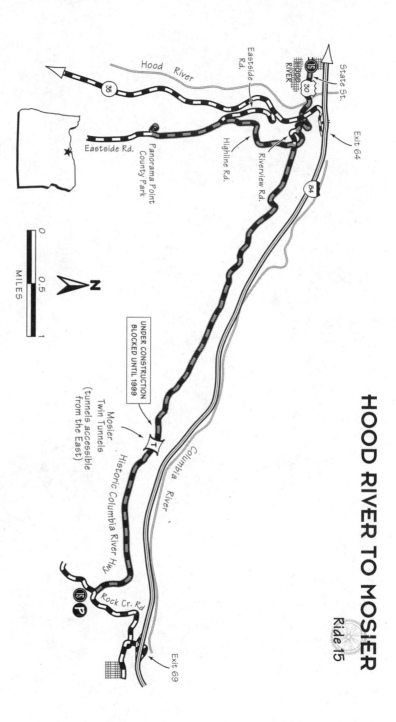

HOOD RIVER TO MOSIER
Ride 15

Hood River

Eastside Rd.

HOOD RIVER

State St.

Exit 64

Eastside Rd.

Panorama Point County Park

Highline Rd.

Riverview Rd.

UNDER CONSTRUCTION
BLOCKED UNTIL 1999

Mosier Twin Tunnels
(tunnels accessible from the East)

Historic Columbia River Hwy

Columbia River

Rock Cr. Rd

Exit 69

MILES

0   0.5   1

N

The Mosier Twin Tunnels on the Historic Columbia River Highway.

The twin tunnels are only 1.5 miles from the parking lot above Mosier, but until construction of the rock sheds is complete in 1999, this is the only way to get into the tunnels. To access the trail from Hood River, park on one of the side

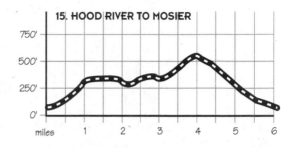

streets downtown. Head east on State Street (US Highway 30) and cross Hood River. A quarter mile beyond the bridge is the intersection with Oregon Highway 35. Ride straight across OR 35 to the Old Columbia River Road (the HCRH) and follow this winding road to the gate near the rock pit. You can follow the HCRH for about three miles past the first gate to the construction area near the Mosier Tunnels. Just before the first gate, Highline Road leads to the south. This road merges with Eastside Road after a mile. Keep heading south on Eastside Road for 0.7 miles to reach Panorama Point County Park.

Sandy Delta

The Sandy River defines the eastern edge of the Portland metropolitan area. Originally named for the quicksand that formed at its mouth, the Sandy River also defines the western boundary of the Columbia River Gorge National Scenic Area. The Forest Service purchased several thousand acres at the mouth of the Sandy River about a decade ago. The low lying plain is covered by cottonwood, blackberry, and reed canary grass. Portions are still grazed, and the Forest Service is trying to control the invasive blackberry and reed canary grass. The shoreline and sloughs harbor waterfowl and shorebirds. Deer, beavers, racoons, and muskrats are common. It is hard to forget that this is a major transportation corridor with barges, airplanes, trains, and highways surrounding the property. Yet, it still feels isolated. The delta has a few miles of shoreline that are rideable when the river is not flooding. While the area is almost flat, the soft surface of the roads forces riders to pedal continuously. After your ride, you may want to visit McMenamin's Edgefield Manor, which is only a few miles away in Troutdale.

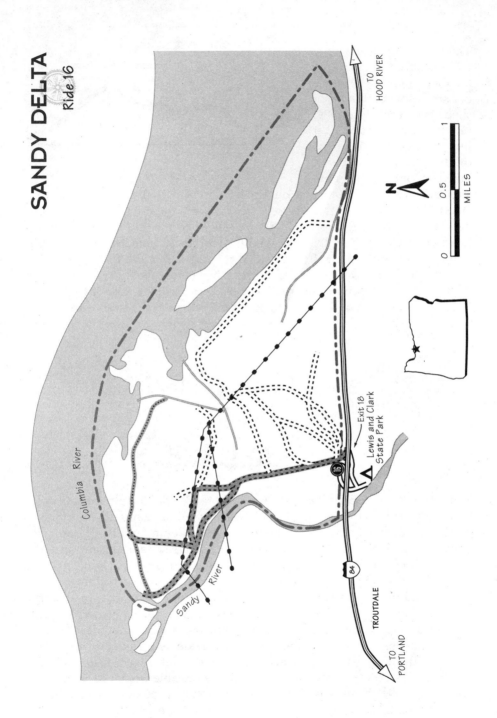

SANDY DELTA
Ride 16

Columbia River

Sandy River

TO
HOOD RIVER

Exit 18
Lewis and Clark
State Park

16

84

TROUTDALE

TO
PORTLAND

N

0   0.5   1
MILES

Edgefield was the county poor farm before it was transformed into a brewery, winery, vineyard, restaurant, movie theater, and hotel.

General location:	On the eastern edge of Portland along the Columbia River.
Distance:	7.8 miles, out and back.
Time:	1 hour.
Aerobic level:	Easy
Elevation change:	Small dips and rises, mostly flat.
Tread:	Gravel and sand roads and doubletracks, closed to motorized vehicles.
Technical difficulty:	2.
Hazards:	Cattle and horses may be encountered. Leave the gates as you find them. Strong winds blow along the Columbia; bring a windbreaker.
Season:	Open and passable all year.
Services:	The freeway exits heading toward Portland offer all services. No drinking water is available at this site.
Rescue index:	Seek help in Troutdale.
Land status:	Columbia River Gorge National Scenic Area, Mt. Hood National Forest.
Maps:	USGS: Washougal.

Sources of additional information: Columbia River Gorge National Scenic Area (see Appendix).

Finding the trail: Take exit 18 from Interstate 84 (the sign says Lewis and Clark State Park). If you are coming from Portland, you need to stay to the

The Sandy Delta on the Columbia River.

right and go back under the interstate. The parking area is just north of the interstate.

THE RIDE

Head north from the parking area, passing several roads leading to the right. After 1.3 miles, the road turns west and runs under high-voltage powerlines for 0.5 mile. Turn north again when the road forks and head to the Columbia River. Ride a mile east along the shore, over deer paths and gravel and sand beach, before a slough blocks your passage. Retrace your route back to the fence you passed just before reaching the beach. Follow the fenceline for 1.7 miles, back to the main north-south road. Head south on the main road back to the parking area or try some of the other roads on the delta.

West Slope Cascades

Wet, rocky, and steep is a good description for most of the singletracks on the west slope of the Cascades. You need balance, strength, and endurance to ride these trails. Take Shellrock Lake to Rock Lake Basin (Ride 17), for example—this is the most difficult ride in the book. I had to walk about half the time. However, it leads to some pretty lakes and seldom-visited old growth stands. An easier ride with spectacular scenery and a small mountain lake runs out Indian Ridge (Ride 18). However, the Indian Ridge Trail is an old road. Portions of the Mollala River Trail system also follow old logging roads, but this complex of trails also includes singletracks that are suitable for intermediate riders. Rain and snow make singletracks impassable for about six months of the year, but the Mollala River area is at lower elevations and has several old roads, so it is open almost year-round. The Ollalie Lake Scenic Area has more than 25 miles of singletrack open to bikes. More than two dozen lakes are scattered across this high-elevation scenic area. The trails in this area are fun, but few riders use them.

Shellrock Lake to Rock Lake Basin

Most of the rides in this book I would do again, and bring a friend—but not this one. This trail is for those who want a real challenge or those who need a humbling experience. Compass and map-reading skills are necessary here, to help you identify the faintest traces of a trail. The lakes warm up enough for swimming by August, and most contain fish. The old-growth forests on the way to Cache Meadow have a quiet mystery that is not found in more popular areas.

General location:	About 40 miles southeast of Portland.
Distance:	11.5 miles, out and back. Or, form a loop by combining Trails 700, 512, and 517.
Time:	2 to3 hours.
Aerobic level:	Strenuous.
Elevation change:	The trail gradually climbs 200 feet to Shellrock Lake; then it climbs 400 feet more to Frazier Turnaround

before dropping 700 feet into the Rock Lake Basin. The trail climbs 300 feet to reach Serene Lake and another 800 feet to reach Trail 517 at the ridgetop. Continuing on the loop, the trail descends 700 feet to Cache Meadows, climbs 700 feet to the junction with Trail 700, and finally descends 800 feet to get back to the trailhead.

Tread: Singletrack in poor condition with numerous downfalls and extremely rocky tread.

Technical difficulty: 5.

Hazards: Extreme conditions for most of the trail. Extremely steep descents, extremely steep ascents, extremely rocky most of the time, and extremely poor maintenance. Be prepared to lift your bike over, under, and around numerous downfalls.

Season: July, August, and September are the only months this trail is likely to be open.

Services: Estacada has most services.

Rescue index: Ripplebrook Guard Station and Government Camp are the nearest places to seek help.

Land status: Estacada Ranger District, Mt. Hood National Forest. The Clackamas and Estacada ranger districts combined after Highway 224 closed.

Maps: The Estacada Ranger District map provides the best information. USGS: Mount Mitchell, High Rock.

Sources of additional information: Mt. Hood National Forest, Estacada Ranger District (see Appendix A).

Finding the trail: After Oregon 224 opens, the quickest route to the trailhead from Portland will be through Estacada. Take Oregon 224 about 27 miles east of Estacada to the Forest Road 57 junction, which is 0.6 miles past Ripplebrook Guard Station. Take a left on Forest Road 57 (paved) for 8.2 miles to the Forest Road 58 junction. Take a left on Forest Road 58 and drive 2.8 miles to the Forest road 5830 junction.

The trailhead to Shellrock Lake is in a clearcut about 5 miles from the 58/5830 junction. The trailhead parking lot is up a small rise on the right about 0.5 mile past the turnoff to Hideaway Lake Campground.

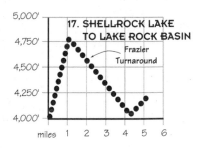

THE RIDE

The trail passes through a clearcut and old growth before reaching Shellrock Lake about 0.5 mile from the trailhead. The rhododendron, bear grass, and fireweed blossoms cover the clearcut in summer, and it produces

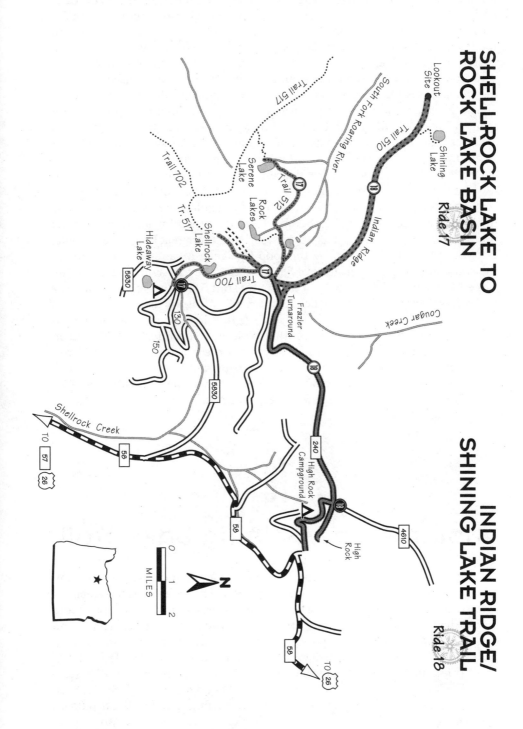

SHELLROCK LAKE TO ROCK LAKE BASIN

INDIAN RIDGE/ SHINING LAKE TRAIL

Lookout Site

Shining Lake

Ride 17

Ride 18

South Fork Roaring River

Trail 517

Trail 510

Trail 512

Trail 702

Tr. 517

17

18

Serene Lake

Rock Lakes

Indian Ridge

Cougar Creek

Shellrock Lake

Hideaway Lake

5830

17

130

150

Trail 700

Frazier Turnaround

18

5830

240

High Rock Campground

High Rock

18

4610

Shellrock Creek

58

TO 57

26

58

58

58

TO 26

MILES

0 1 2

N

71

huckleberries in late August. The trail crosses the outlet of Shellrock Lake and passes through several campsites before starting the climb to Frazier Turnaround. The trail from Shellrock Lake to Frazier Turnaround is not maintained. A small wooden sign (easy to miss) in a campsite on the north-eastern edge of the lake points to the trail, but the trail soon becomes a scramble up a rocky streambed. Talus slopes prevent you from veering too far west on this scramble. After traveling from the lake almost due north for about 0.4 mile, the trail levels off slightly, but the downfalls prevent you from riding until you reach the junction with Trail 517. Take a right down Trail 517 and ride a short distance to Frazier Turnaround. Trail 512 starts behind a sign on the west side of the large parking area.

Trail 512 begins with a quick descent to the junctions leading to Lower, Middle, and Upper Rock lakes. Serene and Middle Rock lakes appear to receive more than Lower Rock Lake. After exploring the short side trails to the Rock lakes, the trail to Serene Lake descends for another 0.5 mile before climbing to Serene Lake. I turned back after reaching Serene Lake, but you may want to complete the loop to Cache Meadows. After passing the campsites on the west shore of Serene Lake, the trail switchbacks up the ridge for about 1 mile to the junction with Trail 517. Turn left on Trail 517 and follow the ridgeline past a helispot. Trail 517 follows the edge of a series of meadows for about 0.5 mile after leaving the ridgetop and passes several trails that lead to the right and eventually merge to become Trail 702. Keep to the left. Trail 517 climbs east, away from the meadows through dense forest. After a long mile of climbing, the trail meets an abandoned road. Turn right on the road and it will lead back to the junction with Trail 700. Take Trail 700 past Shellrock Lake to the trailhead.

See Map on Page 71

Indian Ridge/Shining Lake Trail

Families may enjoy this ride along Indian Ridge, which rises more than 2,000 feet above two forks of the Roaring River. The valleys are too steep for logging roads, so an unbroken forest canopy covers thousands of acres. From an old fire-lookout site at the end of the ridge, you look west to Portland and the Coast Range. This ride is a pleasant alternative to the torturous Rock Lake Basin Loop and it provides spectacular views. Pink rhododendrons greet riders in July, while fireweed and bear grass appear later in the summer. Huckleberries ripen by the end of August and last through September. The north shore of Shining Lake is a good swimming spot, but the trip down is too steep for most cyclists. The ridgeline offers several picnic and camping sites. The site near the trail to Shining Lake has a picnic table.

General location:	About 40 miles southeast of Portland.
Distance:	17.1 miles, out and back from Forest Road 4610.
Time:	1 to 2 hours.
Aerobic level:	Easy.
Elevation change:	The beginning elevation near High Rock is 4,600 feet. The elevation at the far end of the trail is 4,300 feet. The road gently climbs and descends about 200 feet between these points.
Tread:	Dirt and gravel road, closed to motorized vehicles beyond Frazier Turnaround.
Technical difficulty:	2.
Hazards:	Watch for vehicles between Frazier Turnaround and High Rock.
Season:	The trail is usually open from July to October.
Services:	Most services are available in Estacada. Drinking water is not available along the trail or at the trailhead.
Rescue index:	Ripplebrook Guard Station and Government Camp are the nearest places to seek help.
Land status:	Mt. Hood National Forest, Estacada Ranger District.
Maps:	The Mt. Hood National Forest recreation map is adequate, but the Clackamas and Estacada Ranger District maps provide more detailed information.

Sources of additional information: Mt. Hood National Forest, Estacada Ranger District (see Appendix A).

Finding the trail: The quickest route to the trailhead from Portland is through Estacada. Take Oregon Highway 224 about 27 miles east of Estacada to the Forest Road 57 junction, which is 0.6 miles past Ripplebrook Guard Station. Take a left on FR 57 (paved) for 8.2 miles to the Forest Road 58

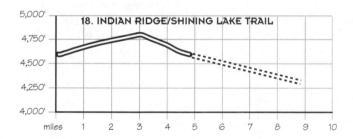

junction. Take a left on FR 58 and drive 5.8 miles to Forest Road 4610. Turn left on Forest Road 4610. Turn left on FR 4610 and travel 1.2 miles to its junction with Road 240. Park at this junction of 4610 and 240 or continue 4.4 miles to Frazier Turnaround. The road to Frazier Turnaround is almost as fast to negotiate on a bike as in a car because it is so rough. It is also more fun on a bike.

The 4.4-mile ride from the junction of Roads 240 and 4610 to Frazier Turn-around has some spectacular views of Mt. Hood and Mt. Jefferson. Just before you reach Frazier Turnaround, a road veers to the right and passes a dispersed campsite. Trail 510 starts about 0.1 mile up this road. A series of berms prevents most vehicles from using the trail. Several short spur roads intersect the trail. About 3.4 miles from the start of the trail, a spur road on the right leads to a picnic/camping area and the trail to Shining Lake. Leave your bike at the top of the mile-long trail to the lake. Indian Ridge ends at a short loop, about 0.7 mile beyond the trail to Shining Lake. Walking beyond the end of the road takes you to the foundation of the Indian Point Lookout and a view down the Roaring River Canyon.

Olallie Scenic Area Loop

Olallie Scenic Area contains thirty-five named lakes and about 25 miles of singletrack that are open to mountain bikes. The dirt road along powerline corridor also offers a challenging ride. The Olallie Scenic Area Loop skirts the southern and eastern boundaries of the scenic area on a rough gravel road before cutting across the middle of the Scenic Area on the Red Lake Trail (Trail 719). The route passes eleven large, named lakes and several smaller unnamed lakes. Breitenbush, Monon, and Olallie lakes provide excellent fishing. My snorkel survey of Top, Sheep, Wall, Averill, and Red lakes indicated that these lakes may be too shallow to sustain fish, but they are sometimes stocked. The lakes were at swimming pool temperature by mid-July. I encountered only one other person while on the Red Lake Trail. **Important Note:** Remember that bikes are not allowed on the Pacific Crest Trail.

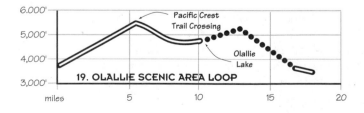

OLALLIE SCENIC AREA LOOP

Ride 19

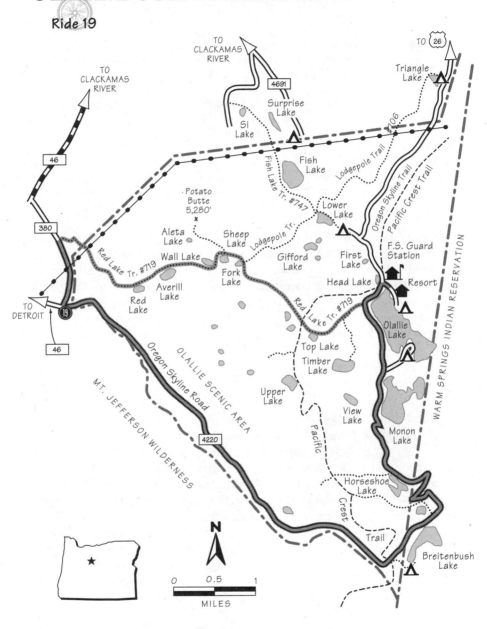

General location:	About 70 miles southeast of Portland.
Distance:	17.8 miles, loop.
Time:	4 hours.
Aerobic level:	Strenuous.
Elevation change:	The ride climbs about 2,300 feet.
Tread:	Rough gravel road for 12.1 miles, rocky singletrack for 5.7 miles.
Technical difficulty:	2 on gravel roads; 4 on singletrack.
Hazards:	Clouds of mosquitoes appear at every stop. Exposed roots and loose cobbles make riding the trail difficult.
Season:	The route is usually open from July to October.
Services:	Olallie Lake Resort has most services.
Rescue index:	Olallie Lake Resort and Guard.
Land status:	Mt. Hood National Forest, Estacada Ranger District.
Maps:	The Estacada Ranger District map provides the best coverage. USGS: Olallie Butte, Mount Jefferson.

Sources of additional information: *The Olallie Scenic Area Guidebook* by Tony George (Solo Press, 1983) is the most complete compilation of information about the area or contact the Mt. Hood National Forest.

Finding the trail: Take Forest Road 46 (paved) from Detroit to the Mt. Hood National Forest boundary, about 23 miles. Turn right (east) on gravel FR 4220 (Oregon Skyline Road). Follow FR 4220 for about 0.4 mile to its junction with FR 380 (gravel) and park on the shoulder.

THE RIDE

The 6-mile climb on Forest Road 4220 to the ridge above Breitenbush Lake is slow enough to make the road's washboard surface unnoticeable. The Pacific Crest Trail crosses the road on this ridge; Olallie Lake is 5.2 miles north from this point. The road passes Breitenbush, Gibson, Horseshoe, and Monon lakes before reaching Olallie Lake. The Red Lake Trail is up a short cutslope, about 0.25 mile before the turnoff to Olallie Lake Resort. The 1929 resort rents cabins and boats and is old enough to be called authentically rustic rather than rundown. In the fifteen minutes it took for me to buy bug repellent at the resort, two 5-pound trout were weighed. The Red Lake Trail has moderate climbs and descents. Almost a third of the 5.7-mile trail consists of cobble-filled ruts, but it is rideable. The trail runs through several marshy areas that are firm enough to ride. Timber Lake Trail takes off to the left after about 0.25 mile. The Pacific Crest Trail crosses the Red Lake Trail about 0.25 mile past Top Lake. The Lodgepole and Potato Butte trails take off to the right near Fork and Sheep lakes, respectively. Stay on the Red Lake Trail.

From Red Lake, the trail descends into larger timber. Downfalls block the trail occasionally. As it crosses under the powerlines, the trail becomes difficult to follow. If you lose it, you can go downhill (west) on the road on the northern edge of the powerline for 0.4 mile to FR 380. A rock cairn marks the trail's junction with the powerline road.

The trail passes through a grove of immense old-growth firs and hemlocks before emerging on FR 380. Turn left (south) on FR 380, and proceed for 0.9 mile back to the parking area on FR 4220.

Mollala River

With the help of volunteers, the Bureau of Land Management has created more than 20 miles of non-motorized trails in the Mollala River Recreation Corridor. Half of the trail system is dirt singletrack through dense stands of young Douglas-fir. Most of the old growth in the Molalla Valley has been cut. The last patches of ragged old trees stand above the young, uniformly conical Douglas-firs. Red alders dominate the riparian areas. The land along the river was recently acquired by the BLM in a land trade with a timber company. The creeks and rivers of the Table Rock and Bull of the Woods wildernesses drain into the Molalla, and the water is cool and clear. The Mollala River has formed dozens of deep holes around car-sized boulders and basalt cliffs. Riders will appreciate these swimming holes on a hot summer day.

General location:	About 9 miles southeast of Molalla.
Distance:	4.4 miles, loop.
Time:	1 hour.
Aerobic level:	Strenuous.
Elevation change:	Fewer than 200 feet.
Tread:	Singletrack for 2.3 miles and doubletrack for 2.1 miles, closed to motorized vehicles.
Technical difficulty:	Mostly 4; some 5.
Hazards:	Watch out for equestrians on the doubletrack.
Season:	The trails are free of snow for most of the year; the singletracks should be ridden only when dry.
Services:	All services available in Molalla.
Rescue index:	Seek help in Molalla.
Land status:	Bureau of Land Management, Salem District.
Maps:	The Salem District of the BLM provides a trail map of the area. USGS: Gawley Creek, Fernwood, Wilhoit.

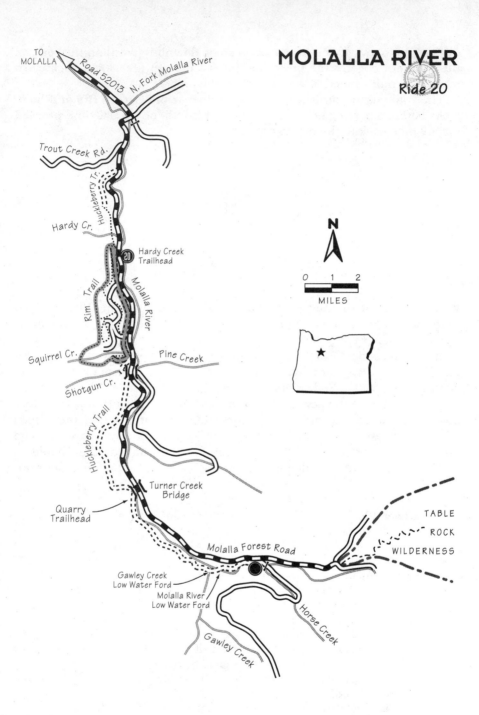

MOLALLA RIVER

Ride 20

N

0   1   2
MILES

TO MOLALLA

Road 52013

N. Fork Molalla River

Trout Creek Rd.

Huckleberry Tr.

Hardy Cr.

20 Hardy Creek Trailhead

Rim Trail

Molalla River

Squirrel Cr.

Pine Creek

Shotgun Cr.

Huckleberry Trail

Turner Creek Bridge

Quarry Trailhead

Molalla Forest Road

Gawley Creek Low Water Ford

Molalla River Low Water Ford

Gawley Creek

Horse Creek

TABLE ROCK WILDERNESS

Sources of additional information: Salem District BLM (see Appendix A).
Finding the trail: From Molalla, head east on Feyrer Park Road. Drive
1.5 miles, past Freyer Park, and cross the Molalla River. Turn right at a
T junction, after crossing the river, and head south to Dickey Prairie. Ride
another 1.5 miles and pass the Dickey Prairie store. Keep heading south on
the Dickie Prairie Road for 4 miles to a cluster of homes known as Glen Avon.
At the southern end of this community, turn right onto the Molalla Forest
Road and cross the Glen Avon Bridge. Keep on the paved road as it turns left
and heads upriver. The Hardy Creek Trailhead is 3 miles past the Glen Avon
Bridge.

THE RIDE

From the Hardy Creek Trailhead, take the doubletrack road uphill for
0.7 mile to the Rim Trail. You cross the Huckleberry Trail, on the way up, at
0.5 mile. The Rim Trail follows the boundary between BLM and private
land for 2.8 miles, through young stands of Douglas-fir and alder. Several
trails lead off to the left from the Rim Trail to meet the Huckleberry Trail.
Stay on the Rim Trail as it dips into Squirrel Creek canyon, 0.25 mile before
intersecting with the Squirrel Creek Tie Trail.

The Squirrel Creek Tie Trail starts as a rough doubletrack. After
0.25 mile, two singletracks branch off from the doubletrack, to the left. The
first track is much more difficult than the second which is 0.1 mile farther
down the road. Ride on the Squirrel Creek Tie Trail for 0.5 mile, to the
Huckleberry Trail, or take one of the singletracks.. Turn left on the Huckleberry Trail for the 2.3-mile ride back to the trailhead.

Opal Creek

This short ride runs through stands of immense Douglas-fir before reaching
the little mining community at Jawbone Flats. The Opal Creek Education
Center has taken over the cluster of buildings at Jawbone Flats and is main-
taining most of the weathered homes, bunkhouses, and shops of the Shiny
Rock Mining Company. Opal Creek gained national attention during the
struggle to preserve local old-growth forests.

In the late 1980s the Detroit District Ranger vowed to clearcut the mountains around Opal Creek, but a determined group of local activists success-
fully blocked the ranger's efforts. The ranger is gone, and the streams still

OPAL CREEK
Ride 21

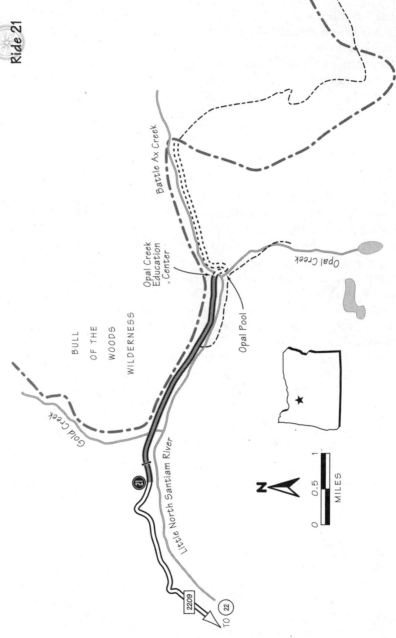

BULL
OF THE
WOODS
WILDERNESS

Battle Ax Creek

Opal Creek
Education
Center

Opal Pool

Opal Creek

Gold Creek

Little North Santiam River

2209

TO 22

N

MILES
0   0.5   1

run clear through the old growth. The area's old-growth forests and cascading streams are remarkable enough to convince many visitors that this area and other old-growth stands deserve to be protected. Thousands of people visit the education center each year. The education center holds Ecology workshops; food and lodging are available for groups.

Abandoned and active mines are scattered along the creeks in the drainage. The mines extracted lead, zinc, copper, silver, and some gold. The road to Jawbone Flats passes several old mine shafts, and mining relics are laid out along the road through the community. Many of the mining claims are still active so obey the No Trespassing signs. Numerous side trails lead from the road to the creeks. Battle Ax Creek, Opal Creek, and the Little North Santiam River race through chasms and tumble over falls into quiet pools that are ideal for swimming during the hottest summer days. The turnaround point for this ride is the short trail to the cliffs above Opal Pool.

General location:	40 miles east of Salem.
Distance:	7.4 miles, out and back.
Time:	1 hour.
Aerobic level:	Easy.
Elevation change:	Small dips and rises, but no significant elevation change.
Tread:	Gravel roads, closed to motorized vehicles.
Technical difficulty:	2.
Hazards:	The bridge decks may be slippery. Watch for people and pets on the road.
Season:	Open and passable almost all year.
Services:	Food and phones are at the junction of the Little North Santiam River Road and Oregon 22. All services are available in Salem.
Rescue index:	Opal Creek Education Center (when staffed). The nearest hospital is in Salem.
Land status:	Willamette National Forest, Detroit Ranger District.
Maps:	The Willamette National Forest recreation map provides adequate coverage. The Detroit Ranger District map provides more information about roads and trails in the area. USGS: Battle Ax.

Sources of additional information: Willamette National Forest, Detroit Ranger District (see Appendix A).

Finding the trail: From Salem, take Oregon 22 east for 17 miles to its junction with the Little North Santiam Road. The Little North Santiam Road is on the north side of the highway, just before OR 22 crosses the Little North Santiam River. The Oregon Department of Forestry office is at the intersection of the Little North Fork Road and Highway 22. Look for a fire danger rating sign. Follow paved Little North Santiam Road for 16 miles to the Willamette National Forest boundary, where the road becomes gravel and changes to Forest Road 2209. The trailhead is 4 miles from the National Forest boundary. Do not block the gate or the road when you park.

Trailhead parking permits are required to park within 0.25 mile of this trailhead. After passing the green gate, the road descends for 0.5 mile to the bridge across Gold Creek. The bridge is about 60 feet above a waterfall and deep pool on Gold Creek. About 1 mile from the trailhead, the road runs along a cliff above the Little North Santiam River. The outer half of the road is a bridge with wooden planking that can be extremely slick when wet. Stay on the gravel part of the road while crossing this long half-bridge. The road rolls up and down through the forest for another 1 mile before coming to the junction with the Opal Creek Trail. The trail is closed to bikes. After 3.1 miles, the road passes through the middle of a cluster of buildings that is the Opal Creek Education Center.

Walk your bike through this rustic mining community. While visitors are welcome, many of the homes are residences, so please respect their privacy. Continue through the town for 0.5 mile to reach the short trail to Opal Pool. Some riders may wish to continue up the steep, rough road that runs along Battle Ax Creek for another 2 miles before coming to the Wilderness boundary. Bikes are not allowed in the Wilderness.

Willamette Valley

Most Oregonians live in the Willamette Valley and it is easy to see why this was the destination for most emigrants. The Willamette's rich soils and mild climate produce the nation's widest array of crops. On the 130-mile drive between Portland and Cottage Grove you pass orchards, berry farms, vineyards, nurseries, row crops, grains, pastures, Christmas tree farms, and grass seed fields. On just about any weekend, you can find a celebration of the valley's crops in one town or another. Finding singletracks in the valley is not as easy. However, Willamette Mission State Park (Ride 22), with its trails through forests and farms, is a good place to start. E. E. Wilson Wildlife Refuge (Ride 23), near Corvallis, doesn't have any singletrack, but it has miles of paved roads that are closed to autos and an interesting collection of pheasants. At the southern end of the valley, the Row River Trail (Ride 24) passes near four of the valley's three dozen covered bridges as it climbs on a converted rail line into the Cascades foothills. All of these trails are suitable for families. While not technically challenging, they give advanced mountain bikers a place to ride when the mountain trails are buried in snow.

Willamette Mission State Park

In 1834, Reverend Jason Lee and four assistants constructed a Methodist mission on the banks of the Willamette River, without which Oregon and Washington could have been part of Canada. By 1834, the Hudson's Bay Company already had a controlling presence in the Pacific Northwest. The British fur trading company had been in the area so long that some of the company's French Canadian fur trappers had retired and established a community on the prairies east of the mission site. The mission's reports attracted other Americans to the valley and by 1843 the Americans had established a provisional government. The Methodists moved the mission to Salem in 1840 because the original site was frequently flooded. The flood of 1861 destroyed the mission buildings and rerouted the Willamette River to its present location.

In addition to its history, the park's other attractions include 4 miles of dirt singletrack, 4 miles of paved trail, a free ferry ride, the nation's largest black cottonwood (9 feet in diameter and 156-feet tall), a pastoral setting, and flocks of geese in the winter. The riparian forest of cottonwood, ash,

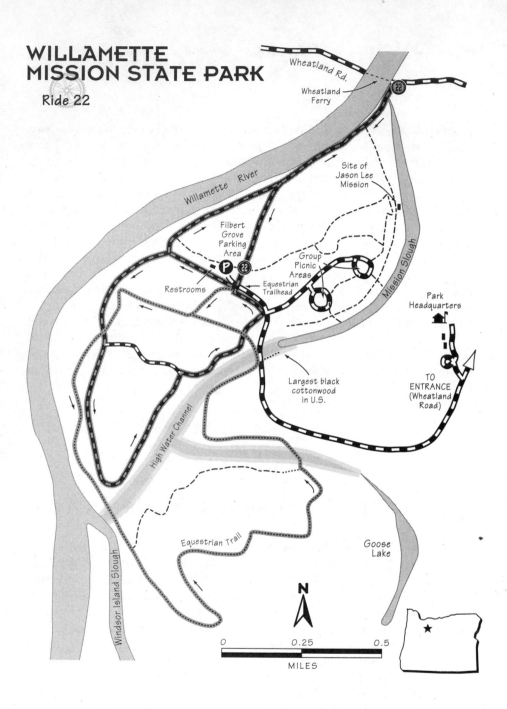

WILLAMETTE
MISSION STATE PARK

Ride 22

Wheatland Rd.

Wheatland Ferry

22

Willamette River

Site of Jason Lee Mission

Filbert Grove Parking Area

Group Picnic Areas

P 22

Restrooms

Equestrian Trailhead

Mission Slough

Park Headquarters

TO ENTRANCE (Wheatland Road)

Largest black cottonwood in U.S.

High Water Channel

Equestrian Trail

Goose Lake

Windsor Island Slough

N

0   0.25   0.5

MILES

and willow harbor a variety of other birds and wildlife. Trails in the park are almost flat, but the soft surface of the singletracks eliminates coasting. The park manager allows bikes on the equestrian trails. Mountain bikers need to yield to equestrians, and please remember: Never spook the horses.

From October through June the river may rise and cover portions of the trails, especially the equestrian loop. A little water on the trail is a challenge, but 3 feet of water on a mud trail left me wading when I did my ride. You will need a day-use ($3.00) or annual State Park permit ($25.00). You can buy these at the entrance.

General location:	9 miles north of Salem.
Distance:	7.4 miles, double loop.
Time:	1 to 2 hours.
Aerobic level:	Easy.
Elevation change:	Less than 100 feet.
Tread:	Paved bike path for 3.6 miles, singletrack for 3.8 miles.
Technical difficulty:	1 on paved trail; 3 on horse trail.
Hazards:	Equestrians use the park frequently; give horses and their riders plenty of room and warning. Watch for other trail users. Water may cover the trails.
Season:	Open and suitable for riding year-round, except when snow and ice cover the trails. Heavy rains make the equestrian trails impassable.
Services:	Salem and Keizer, 9 miles south, have all services.
Rescue index:	Salem is the best place to seek medical attention, but emergencies may also be reported to the park headquarters.
Land status:	Oregon Parks and Recreation Department.
Maps:	The park provides a map of the trails. USGS: Mission Bottom.

Sources of additional information: Oregon Parks and Recreation Department (see Appendix).

Finding the trail: The entrance to the park is 9 miles north of Salem or 4.5 miles from the Brook exit on Interstate 5 (exit 263). From the Brook exit, head west on Brooklake Road for 2 miles to Wheatland Road. Go north on Wheatland Road for 2.5 miles to the park entrance. Drive into the park to the Filbert Grove Day Use Area.

THE RIDE

From the Filbert Grove parking area, head toward the river (west) on the paved trail. Turn north (down stream) when the trail forks and ride 1 mile to the Wheatland Ferry. Bicyclists and pedestrians may ride the ferry back and forth across the Willamette for free. Return on the same paved trail for

The Wheatland Ferry on the Willamette River.

0.7 mile and take a left on the paved trail when the trail forks through the Filbert Orchard. Follow this past the Filbert Grove parking area and follow it west to the river again (this is the same trail you started on). Turn left (up-stream) at the junction this time and follow this trail around to the equestrian trailhead. You can stay on the paved trail at this point or go right (west) on the equestrian trail. The paved trail will bring you back to the parking area. If you choose the equestrian singletrack, head west until it turns south and runs along the Willamette River. After dropping in and out of a swale, the trail leaves the river, cuts through a forest and emerges on the edge of a farm field. Follow the western and northern edges of the field until the trail leads into the forest. The trail crosses another swale before emerging on another farm field. Follow the trail west around this field and back to the trailhead.

E.E. Wilson Wildlife Area

This World War II military training center contains a diversity of valley habitats, which harbor numerous species of wildlife. A few months after

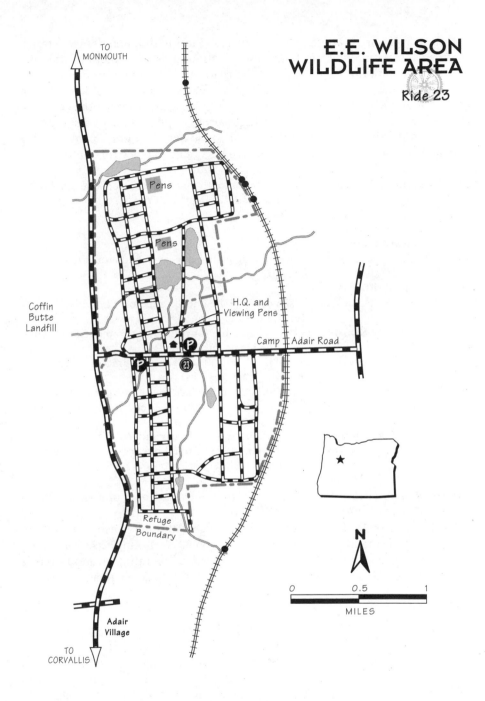

E.E. WILSON
WILDLIFE AREA
Ride 23

TO
MONMOUTH

Pens

Pens

Coffin
Butte
Landfill

H.Q. and
Viewing Pens

Camp Adair Road

23

Refuge
Boundary

Adair
Village

TO
CORVALLIS

N

0   0.5   1
MILES

World War II started, more than 1,600 acres of farms and marshes were transformed into a small city to house tens of thousands of soldiers in training. Most of the buildings are gone, but the roads and building foundations provide an eerie reminder of the areas history. The Oregon Department of Fish and Wildlife (ODFW) raises pheasants and other game birds in the center of the refuge and they have an interesting variety of pheasants on display near the main parking area. The network of roads here is a great place to play cat-and-mouse with a group of cyclists. This is a good place for a family ride.

General location:	Between Monmouth and Corvallis, off Oregon 99W.
Distance:	16 miles (total distance of all roads).
Time:	1 to 2 hours.
Aerobic level:	Easy.
Elevation change:	Almost flat.
Tread:	Gravel and asphalt roads, closed to motorized vehicles.
Technical difficulty:	2.
Hazards:	Poison oak may be encountered off the trails. Hunters use the area.
Season:	Open and suitable for riding year-round, except when snow and ice cover the roads.
Services:	Corvallis, 11 miles south, and Monmouth, 11 miles north, have all services.
Rescue index:	Corvallis is the best place to seek medical attention, but emergencies may also be reported to the refuge headquarters.
Land status:	Oregon Department of Fish and Wildlife.
Maps:	The Lewisburg USGS quad map covers the area and shows the road network.

Sources of additional information: Oregon Department of Fish and Wildlife (see Appendix A).

Finding the trail: The entrance to the refuge is 2 miles north of Adair Village or 11 miles south of Monmouth on Oregon 99W. Parking areas line Camp Adair Road beginning 0.125 mile east of OR 99W. The refuge headquarters is 0.5 mile from Highway 99 on the north side of Camp Adair Road.

THE RIDE

Park at the main parking area, about 0.5 mile from Highway 99W. Interpretive signs explain the history of the area. The road heading north passes pens that contain several varieties of pheasant. Basically, you can pick your own route when exploring the refuge. The loop around the outer edge is about 6 miles long and crosses Camp Adair Road twice. You can add distance and variety to the ride by doing concentrically smaller loops and riding the short connecting roads. The refuge has a small lake north of the headquarters. Some of the side roads have overgrown to become single tracks.

Row River Trail

The Bureau of Land Management acquired this former rail line in 1994 and completed work on the trail in 1996. The trail crosses two interesting iron bridges and passes near four covered bridges. The hard-surfaced path makes for easy biking and is suitable for riders with basic riding skills of all ages. The Oregon Pacific and Eastern Railroad was constructed in 1902, to haul gold-bearing ore from the Bohemia mines and lumber from the Culp Creek Mill. The line carried tourists as well as lumber in the 1970s and 1980s, but it was abandoned shortly after the mill at Culp Creek burned. Several movies were filmed along the route, including *Stand by Me*, starring River Phoenix. The ride through pastures and forests along Dorena Lake and the Row River is a peaceful retreat. On hot summer days, swimming in the lake or under the bridges is hard to resist. On rainy days, the covered bridges provide shelter for picnics.

General location:	3 miles east of Cottage Grove.
Distance:	28.5 miles (30.9 miles if you ride to Stewart Covered Bridge), out and back.
Time:	3 to 4 hours.
Aerobic level:	An easy ride, but the length allows even experienced riders to get a workout.
Elevation change:	The trail climbs the 300 feet from Mosby Creek to Culp Creek almost imperceptibly.
Tread:	Excellent packed gravel–asphalt surface on a wide trail.
Technical difficulty:	1.
Hazards:	Watch for other trail users and yield the right of way.
Season:	Open year-round and passable except during periods of snow and ice.
Services:	Cottage Grove has all services.
Rescue index:	Help is available in Cottage Grove.
Land status:	Bureau of Land Management.
Maps:	USGS 7.5 minute quad: Dorena Lake. The trail is identified on the quad map as a railroad. The free BLM map of the trail is adequate.

Sources of additional information: Bureau of Land Management (see Appendix A).

Finding the trail: Take exit 174 from I-5 and head east on the Row River Road. About 0.25 mile east of the interstate, turn right on Thornton Road. Thornton Road hits Mosby Creek Road after 0.125 mile. Turn left (east) and follow Mosby Creek Road for about 2 miles to the trailhead next to the

ROW RIVER TRAIL
Ride 24

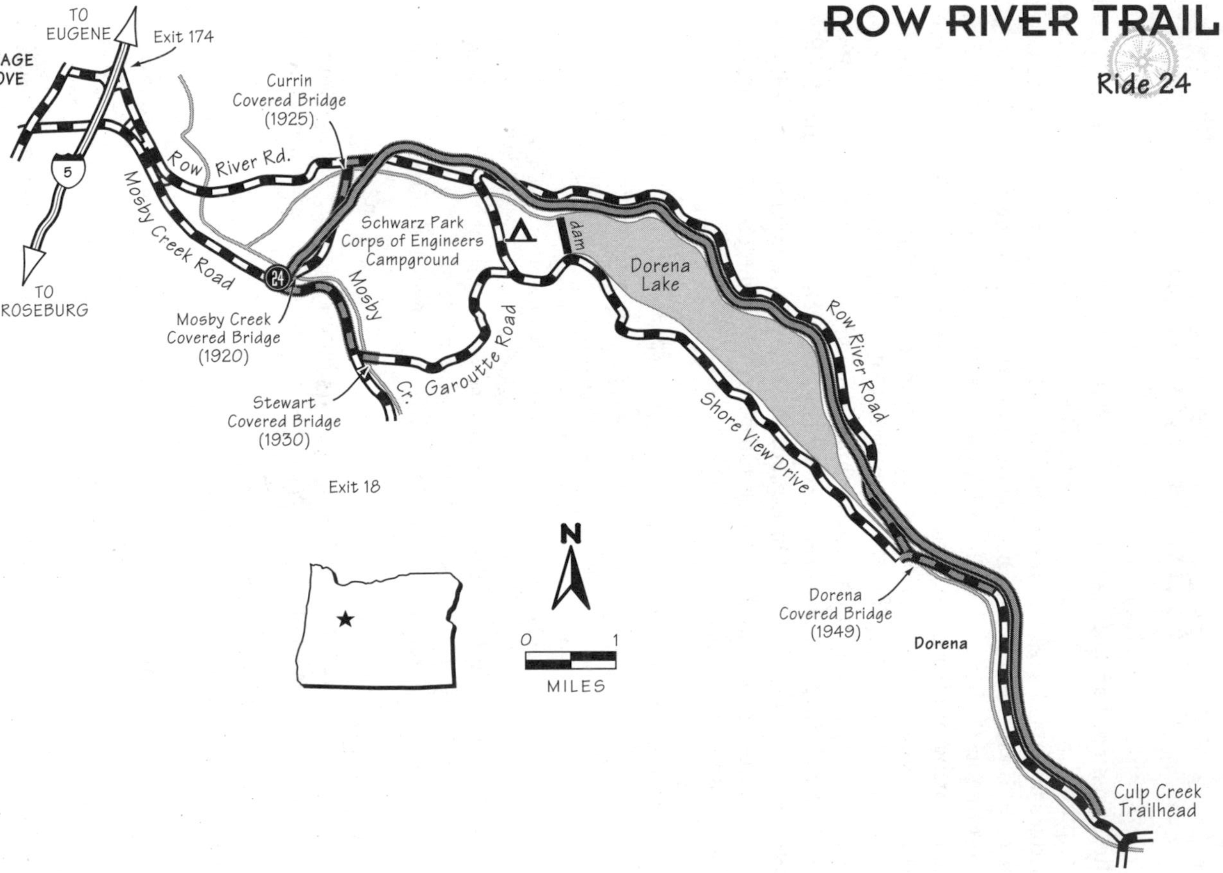

Culp Creek Trailhead

Row River Road

Dorena

Dorena Covered Bridge (1949)

Dorena Lake

Shore View Drive

dam

Schwarz Park Corps of Engineers Campground

Garoutte Road

Currin Covered Bridge (1925)

Row River Rd.

Mosby

Cr.

Mosby Creek Covered Bridge (1920)

Stewart Covered Bridge (1930)

Exit 18

24

Mosby Creek Road

Exit 174

TO EUGENE

COTTAGE GROVE

5

TO ROSEBURG

N

0   1
MILES

The Dorena Covered Bridge over the Row River.

Mosby Creek Covered Bridge. The parking area for the trail is near the red iron bridge.

THE RIDE

The Row River Trail passes three covered bridges, but you must leave the trail to cross them. The fourth bridge is a mile east of the trailhead on Mosby Creek Road. The Currin Covered Bridge (1925) crosses the

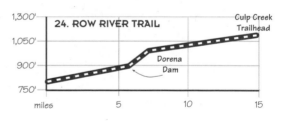

Row River about 2 miles north of the trailhead. The bridge is visible from the trail and only a short distance west on the Row River Road. The Currin Covered Bridge is closed to traffic, but the local folks hold square dances on the bridge almost every Saturday afternoon during the summer. The steepest part of the trail is the 3-percent climb to the top of Dorena Dam. The trail runs along the shore of Dorena Lake and crosses the Row River Road at the eastern end of the lake. If you get off the trail and follow the road for 0.9 mile, you pass the Dorena Covered Bridge (1932). Continue east on the Row River Road for another 0.4 mile, the trail is adjacent to the road. Get

From the Row River Railroad Bridge, the Currin Covered Bridge can be seen in the distance. Square dances are held inside the Currin Bridge on most summer Saturdays.

back on the trail for the ride to Culp Creek Trailhead. The slightly descending grade makes the cycling much easier on the ride back to the trailhead. If you still have the energy left when you reach Mosby Creek, ride another 1 mile east on the Mosby Creek Road to Garoutte Road and Stewart Covered Bridge (1930).

Southwest Oregon

Hot dry summers and mild winters allow the forests in Southwest Oregon's Klamath, Siskiyou, and Cascade mountains to support different species of trees than those found in Northwest Oregon. Incense cedar, sugar pine, Port Orford cedar, and redwood begin to replace Douglas-fir and western hemlock—the most common trees in Northwest Oregon forests. In Southwest Oregon, south-facing slopes are grasslands; they are too dry to support forests. Here, wildlife diversity and density is the highest in Oregon.

The Dunning Ranch provides habitat for several rare species, including Columbian white-tailed deer. Ride 25 introduces mountain bikers to the grasslands and forests that allow the deer to thrive along the North Umpqua River. Stay on the roads in this refuge to avoid frightening the deer and coming into contact with poison oak. Farther upstream on the North Umpqua River, Ride 26 on the North Umpqua Trail is a glide through dense forest on cool, north-facing slopes. The North Umpqua Trail dips and climbs for 79 miles, following the river to its source.

Ride 27 starts at the almost-forgotten east entrance to Crater Lake National Park. This route to the rim of Crater Lake passes dozens of weird pinnacles rising 100 feet from Sand Creek Canyon. On the plains east of the Cascades, Ride 28 follows the old OC & E railroad line through marshes and deserts between Klamath Falls and Bly. The bird life along the Sprague River–segment of this ride is awesome, so bring your binoculars! The Weyerhauser Timber Company added the Wood Line Branch to the OC & E in 1940; this old railbed is now a great 51-mile mountain bike ride (Ride 29). The Forest Service (with help from volunteers) is retrofitting the trestles in this rail-to-trail State Park for safer biking.

Dunning Ranch

For years, I've enjoyed rolling through the grass-covered hills of Western Oregon. The gentle curves, tanned by late summer, lead to hidden valleys darkened by brush and forest. Exploring these seductive hills has never been more pleasant than the time I visited the Dunning Ranch. On these hills overlooking the North Umpqua River, I was able to glide for miles through meadows and forest. The BLM named this 6,900 acres the North

DUNNING RANCH
Ride 25

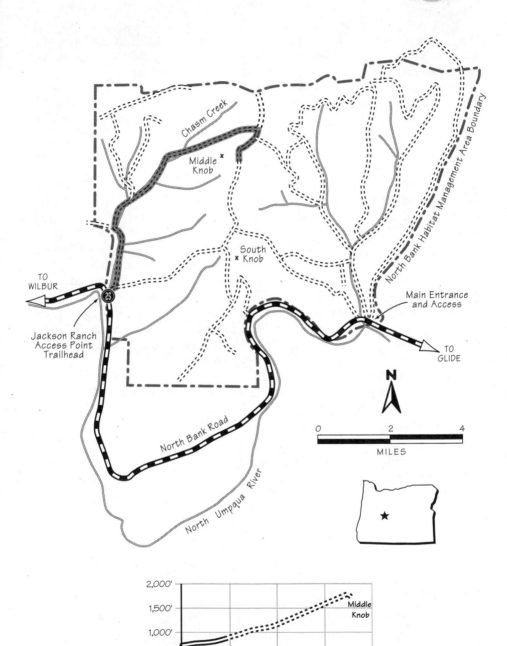

Chasm Creek

Middle ✗ Knob

North Bank Habitat Management Area Boundary

South ✗ Knob

TO WILBUR

Main Entrance and Access

Jackson Ranch Access Point Trailhead

TO GLIDE

25

North Bank Road

North Umpqua River

N

| 0 | | 2 | | 4 |
MILES

★

2,000'

1,500'

1,000'

Middle Knob

500'

0'

25. DUNNING RANCH

miles   1   2   3   4

You can ride the ridgetops at the Dunning Ranch.

Bank Habitat Management Area. Most locals call it the Dunning Ranch, a much easier reference. The BLM manages the area for the endangered Columbian white-tailed deer. The mixture of rolling grasslands with oak and fir trees in the draws provides ideal habitat for deer, and spectacular, scenic mountain biking for intermediate and advanced cyclists.

General location: About 10 miles northeast of Roseburg on the North Umpqua River.

Distance: 7.2 miles, out and back.

Time: 1 to 2 hours.

Aerobic level: Strenuous.

Elevation change: From 560 feet elevation at the Jackson Ranch Access, the trail climbs about 1,000 feet to reach Middle Knob.

Tread: Grass-covered roads in good condition (but sometimes hard to follow).

Technical difficulty: 4.

Hazards: Poison oak, chiggers, and ticks are abundant, but rattlesnakes are rare. When the grassy roads are wet from dew or rain, descents become frightening.

Season: The ranch is open year-round for non-motorized use, but the roads may become impassible due to mud or snow.

Services: Most services are available in Wilbur. Roseburg has all services.

Rescue index:	Help may be found in Wilbur or Roseburg.
Land status:	Bureau of Land Management
Maps:	Free brochures are available from the Roseburg BLM Office. USGS: Oak Creek Valley (does not display the road network).

Sources of additional information: Bureau of Land Management; Roseburg District (see Appendix A).

Finding the trail: Take exit 129 or 134 from Interstate 84 and follow Oregon 99 to the town of Wilbur. The North Bank Road intersects OR 99 near the aluminum plant. Follow the North Bank Road east for 5.3 miles to the Jackson Ranch Access. The highway shoulder near the signed and gated road is wide enough to park on without blocking the road. Access is also available at mile points 10.3 and 12.3 along the North Bank Road.

THE RIDE

After going through the gate, follow the well-maintained gravel road about 1.5 miles until it crosses a small creek and a road on the right. You leave BLM land if you continue on the main gravel road another 0.5 mile. The right fork follows Chasm Creek through pastures and oak forests, becoming progressively more overgrown until it almost disappears after it crosses the creek. The road becomes visible again as you ride uphill through the meadow. If you lose the road in the meadow along the creek, look uphill for the cleared passage through the forest or the roadcut on the hillside to the northeast. The loose gravel and steep grade make riding the last 0.5 mile to the ridgetop almost impossible. You can go either north or south at the ridgetop. I went north to the property line, then doubled back to climb Middle Knob. This route has several obvious loop alternatives to be explored.

The North Umpqua Trail: Tioga Segment

Along the Tioga Segment of the North Umpqua Trail, the North Umpqua River is a series of deep pools separated by short falls and rapids. Renowned for its exceptional fishing, the area receives only moderate use from other recreationists. From Swiftwater Trailhead, a short gravel path leads to the Deadline Falls overlook where you can watch salmon leap the falls on their

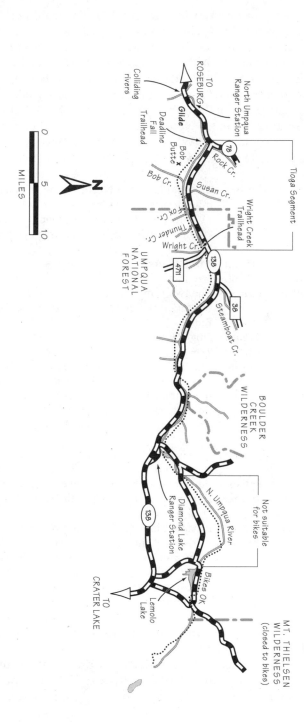

NORTH UMPQUA TRAIL OVERVIEW

Colliding rivers

TO ROSEBURG

North Umpqua Ranger Station

Glide

Deadline Fall Trailhead

Bob Butte ✗

Bob Cr.

Rock Cr.

Susan Cr.

78

Tioga Segment

Fox Cr.

Thunder Cr.

Wright Cr.

Wright Creek Trailhead

138

4711

38

Steamboat Cr.

UMPQUA NATIONAL FOREST

BOULDER CREEK WILDERNESS

Not suitable for bikes

N. Umpqua River

Diamond Lake Ranger Station

138

Bikes Ok

Lemolo Lake

TO CRATER LAKE

MT. THIELSEN WILDERNESS (closed to bikes)

MILES

0   5   10

N

way upstream to spawn from June to October. The trail then leads through a stand of old-growth Douglas-fir and cedar with a sword-fern understory. The first 5 miles on the west end of the Tioga Segment are fairly flat and suitable for beginning cyclists. For the more experienced riders, I recommend starting at Wright Creek. The trail over Bob Butte from the east is too steep to ascend or descend for all but the most advanced riders, but it is short. The more gradual grade of the trail on the west side of Bob Butte allows riders a long and exciting descent. Several steep side trails lead to isolated riverside campsites next to quiet pools. While the Umpqua is never warm, on hot days you might appreciate a quick dip in the pools after your ride.

General location:	The trail is on the North Umpqua River, about 30 miles east of Roseburg.
Distance:	31.4 miles, out and back or loop. (57 miles of the 79-mile North Umpqua Trail are open to mountain bikes.)
Time:	4 to 5 hours.
Aerobic level:	Strenuous.
Elevation change:	The two trailheads are almost at the same elevation, but the trail climbs about 500 feet to get over Bob Butte.
Tread:	Singletrack.
Technical difficulty:	4.
Hazards:	The trail includes a few tight turns and narrow sections along cliffs. The bridges are slippery even when the trail is dry. Be prepared to ride or walk through patches of poison oak that overgrow the trail. The highway has narrow shoulders and moderate traffic.
Season:	This is a dry season trail, but it may be free of snow year-round
Services:	Ildeyld Park and Glide have most services.
Rescue index:	Help may be available at the Ranger Station in Glide or in Roseburg.
Land status:	Private, BLM, and Umpqua National Forest.
Maps:	A free map that describes trail segments and provides other useful information is available from BLM and Forest Service offices listed in Appendix A or at the Colliding Rivers Visitor Center in Glide. USGS: Steamboat, Mace Mountain, Old Fairview.

Sources of additional information: Bureau of Land Management; Umpqua National Forest (see Appendix).

Finding the trail: The western trailhead begins on the south side of the North Umpqua River at the BLM's Swiftwater Trailhead or the adjoining Swiftwater County Park. Swiftwater Bridge is 6 miles east of Glide on Oregon 138.

The North Umpqua River.

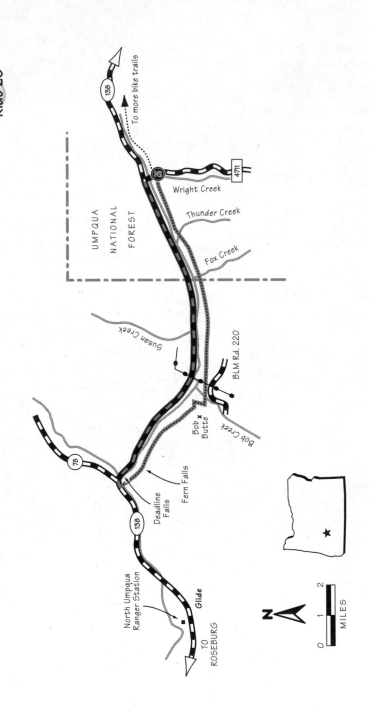

NORTH UMPQUA TRAIL: TIOGA SEGMENT

Ride 26

To more bike trails

138

138

4711

Wright Creek

Thunder Creek

UMPQUA NATIONAL FOREST

Fox Creek

Susan Creek

BLM Rd. 220

Bob Butte

Bob Creek

78

Fern Falls

Deadline Falls

138

North Umpqua Ranger Station

Glide

TO ROSEBURG

N

MILES

0   1   2

The Forest Service recently cleared the Tioga segment of the North Umpqua Trail.

The eastern access to this section of the trail is at Wright Creek, which is 11.7 miles farther east on Oregon 138. The Wright Creek Trailhead has a large parking area on the south side of the bridge.

THE RIDE

From Wright Creek Bridge, the trail has some moderate climbs and descents through fir and cedar forest. The dense canopy discourages poison oak. A few steep side trails lead down to the Umpqua. Keep track of your location by noting the major stream crossings, which are bridged. Before climbing Bob Butte, the trail uses an old logging road for about 1 mile. The first segment of logging road is flat and closed to motorized vehicles. The second segment, closer to Bobs Butte, has a new gravel surface and is open to

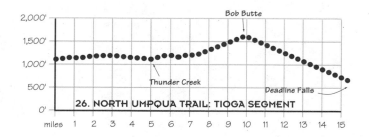

vehicles. The exit from this segment back to the trail was not marked, so watch for the trail on the right. The trail drops to a small creek before starting a long steep ascent around Bob Butte. The rocky outcrops and cliffs receive more sunlight than the beginning of the trail, which encourages poison oak to cover the trail. The descent from Bob Butte is more gradual than the ascent. The trail then passes through an old-growth Douglas-fir stand with trees 5 feet in diameter and larger. This glide toward Glide receives more use as the trail approaches Swiftwater Trailhead. For a quick return to the Wright Creek Bridge, take Highway 138. Most of the highway has a narrow shoulder, but traffic is usually light.

Crater Lake: East Entrance

Crater Lake National Park is becoming more popular for bicycling, but the narrow, shoulderless Rim Drive is crowded with vehicles during the summer. The continual fear of being rear-ended or forced off cliffs is distracting when trying to appreciate America's deepest lake. Accessing the rim via the

The Phantom Ship formation in Crater Lake

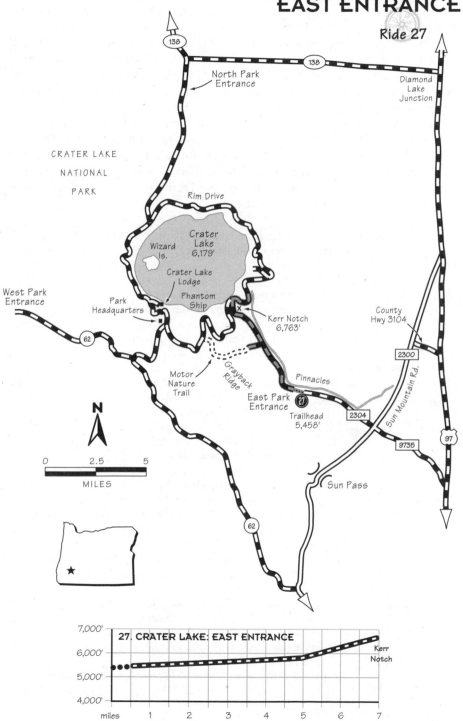

CRATER LAKE: EAST ENTRANCE

Ride 27

138

North Park
Entrance

138

Diamond
Lake
Junction

CRATER LAKE

NATIONAL

PARK

Rim Drive

Crater
Lake
6,179'

Wizard
Is.

Crater Lake
Lodge

Phantom
Ship

West Park
Entrance

Park
Headquarters

Kerr Notch
6,763'

County
Hwy 3104

62

2300

Motor
Nature
Trail

Grayback
Ridge

Pinnacles

East Park
Entrance

27

Trailhead
5,458'

2304

Sun Mountain Rd.

9735

97

N

0   2.5   5
MILES

Sun Pass

62

27. CRATER LAKE: EAST ENTRANCE

7,000'

6,000'

Kerr
Notch

5,000'

4,000'

miles   1   2   3   4   5   6   7

forgotten East Entrance to the park (Pinnacles Road) avoids travel on Rim Drive, and takes you past the bizarre 100-foot tall pumice pinnacles, which are overlooked by most park visitors. If you try this route just before Rim Drive opens, you will have the 6-mile Pinnacles Road to yourself. You can experience the change in season from mid-summer to winter by ascending only 1,300 feet on the two-lane paved road. Pinnacles Road hits Rim Drive only a few hundred feet from the Phantom Rock Overlook, which was designed for picnicking. The return descent on the empty road was steep enough to be exhilarating without being frightening. Because I did this ride early in the season, I had to walk across intermittent snowdrifts to reach the rim. Coming back down I was able to ride on top of many of the drifts. This is a long climb at high altitude and can be strenuous if aggressively ridden, but the moderate grade is easy if taken slowly. It is suitable for beginning riders. The sand and dirt Grayback Motor Nature Trail offers an alternative route to the rim, but is snow-covered until mid-July.

General location:	Crater Lake National Park in Southwest Oregon.
Distance:	14 miles, out and back.
Time:	2 hours.
Aerobic level:	Moderate.
Elevation change:	The road climbs 1,300 feet from the Pinnacles Overlook to Kerr Notch on the rim of Crater Lake.
Tread:	The first 0.25 mile is a gravel path. The rest is paved, but if traveled early in the summer, portions will be snow-covered.
Technical difficulty:	2.
Season:	June through October. To avoid automobiles, use this route during the 2-to-3-week period between the opening of the North Entrance and the opening of Rim Drive. The Pinnacles Road should be clear to Kerr Notch except for some snowdrifts near the rim. The North Entrance is usually open by Memorial Day, but Rim Drive may be closed until mid-July. Snow closes Rim Drive by November. This route may also be used when all the roads are open.
Services:	The nearest services to the east entrance are 25 miles north at the junction of Oregon Highway 138 and US Highway 97 (Diamond Lake Junction).
Hazards:	The sandy slopes above Pinnacle Valley and on the rim of Crater Lake are very unstable; stay back from the edge.
Rescue index:	When Rim Drive is open, the park headquarters is 11.4 miles clockwise around the rim from Kerr Notch. Otherwise, seek help at Diamond Lake Junction.
Land status:	Crater Lake National Park and Winema National Forest.
Maps:	The Winema National Forest recreation map is adequate for this trip. USGS: Crater Lake East, Sun Pass.

The Pinnacles in Crater Lake National Park.

Sources of additional information: Crater Lake National Park (see Appendix).

Finding the trail: From Bend, take U.S. Highway 97 for 70 miles south to the junction with Oregon 138 (Diamond Lake Junction). Three miles south of Diamond Lake Junction on US 97, turn right on the Sun Mountain Road (Forest Road 2300). Follow the cinder-covered Sun Mountain Road for 15 miles to its junction with Forest Road 2304. A sign indicates that this is the way to the Pinnacles Trail. The trailhead is in a clearcut about 4.5 miles from FR 2300.

THE RIDE

The trail runs along the edge of the clearcut until it reaches a huge sign announcing the East Entrance to the park. The trail reaches a paved road after bringing riders precariously close to cliffs above the Pinnacles. Follow the paved road 6.5 miles to Kerr Ridge. Phantom Rock Overlook is 100 yards to the right on Rim Drive. Continue up Rim Drive for views toward Klamath Marsh.

Alternate routes: You can make a loop trip later in the summer by taking the Grayback Motor Trail to Rim Drive and then descending on the Pinnacles Road. This requires riding on Rim Drive for only 5.6 miles.

OC & E Woods Line State Trail: Bly to Klamath Falls

This rail-to-trail offers more wildlife-viewing opportunities than any other trail in this book. The section between Bly and Sprague River is a birder's paradise. The OC & E Line carried logs and lumber between Klamath Falls and Bly from 1927 until the 1980s. Oregon State Parks and Recreation acquired the line in 1992. Gradually, through grants and the hard work of many volunteers, the trail is being improved. The paved and graded sections near Klamath Falls are the most popular. Between Olene and Bly the rough, loose gravel surface discourages intensive use, but offers solitude and a tremendous workout. Even powerhouse pedalers will perspire profusely as they propel themselves along the perpetual 2 percent grade and over the pass at Switchback Hill.

My hands grew numb from rattling over the gravel and my thighs and calves went into spasms from exertion, but I am eager to take this ride again. West of Bly, where marshes line both sides of the trail, the sounds of waterfowl calling and rising from the water were continuous. Pelicans, herons, egrets, cranes, hawks, and vultures startled me as they took off so close, I could hear feather brush feather. Coyote packs barked in defense of their dens. A beaver swimming below the surface kept pace with me for a short distance before diving deeper and out of sight. A half-dozen circling Vs of geese told me I was approaching Smokey Lake, which was crowded with rafts of waterfowl. My singing mesmerized cud-chewing herds as I passed, and I came to appreciate every soft deposit the horses and cattle had made on the course gravel surface of the trail. This trail can be ridden in shorter segments than the one described here.

General location:	The trail runs from Klamath Falls to Bly in Southwest Oregon.
Distance:	63.3 miles, one way.
Time:	10 hours.
Aerobic level:	Easy to strenuous depending on the section traveled.
Elevation change:	The trail ascends 600-foot Switchback Hill at a gradual 2-to-3-percent grade. The grade is continuous for about 6 miles coming from either direction. The trail is almost flat the rest of the way.
Tread:	Starting in Klamath Falls, the first 3.3 miles are paved. The next 3.8 miles are rolled gravel. The 24.2 miles between Olene and Switchback Hill are packed and loose basalt. The 32 miles from the switchbacks to Bly are mostly loose basalt.
Technical difficulty:	1 through the paved section; 2 on rolled gravel; 3 on loose basalt.
Hazards:	The trestles over the Sprague River did not have decks in 1997, but they are scheduled for decking in 1998. If not decked, they are easy to walk, but hard to ride. Riders rarely see rattlesnakes. Bring plenty of water, it is a long way between towns. One gallon was not enough for my mid-summer ride.
Season:	The trail is open year-round. While the Switchback Hill area may be blocked by snow and ice most of the winter, other sections may be open during thaws or mild winters.
Services:	All services are available in Klamath Falls. Dairy, Sprague River, Beatty, and Bly have cafes and convenience stores.
Rescue index:	Help may be obtained in Klamath Falls or in the small towns along the route.
Land status:	The rail line is a state park.
Maps:	Call the Oregon State Parks and Recreation Department for a free trail map. Other maps include the Winema National Forest map and USGS: Klamath Falls, Altamont, Dairy, Swan Lake, Yonina, Sprague River West, Sprague River East, Beatty, Feguson Mountain, and Bly.

OC & E WOODS LINE STATE TRAIL: BLY TO KLAMATH FALLS

Ride 28

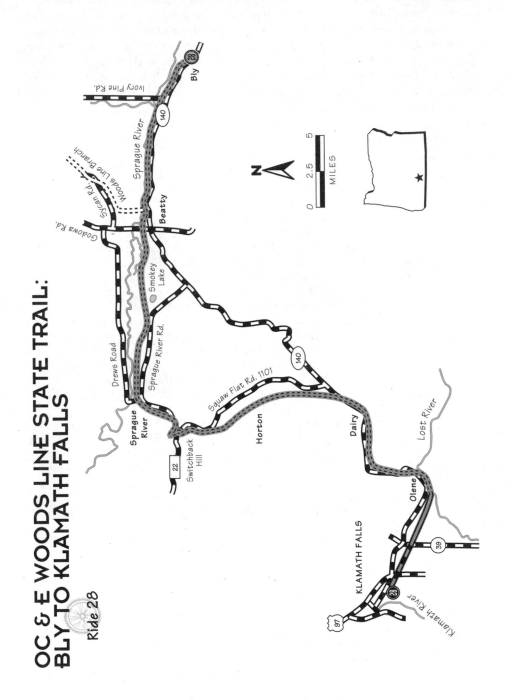

Numerous trestles cross the Sprague River west of Bly.

Sources of additional information: Oregon State Parks and Recreation Department (see Appendix).

Finding the trail: The trailhead is 1.7 miles southeast of downtown Klamath Falls and the Klamath County Court House. Take Oregon 39 from downtown to Washburn Way. Turn right on Washburn, and then turn left at the next light (Crosby Avenue). The trailead is 0.25 mile on the left. A second trailhead is located farthereast on OR 39 (South 6th Street) about 0.25 mile south of the OR 39 and Oregon 140 intersection. The trail is also accessible at any of the numerous road crossings along the route where parking may be available along the shoulder. To access the trail in Bly, park at the U.S. Forest Service Station and ride on OR 140 until it intersects the rail line or follow Marvin Avenue, which dead-ends at the rail line. The rail line runs through an old mill site in Bly and may be a little hard to follow. Be sure to leave all gates as you find them (open or closed) as you leave town.

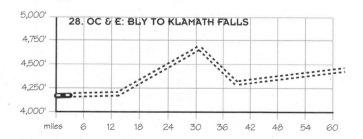

The flat section between Bly and Sprague River follows the Sprague River through marshes, desert, pasture, and by Smokey Lake. The loose gravel surface along most of the route makes pedaling difficult. About 11 miles from Bly, the Wood Line Branch heads north toward Sycan Siding. The Woods Line Branch is described in Ride 29. The trail enters ponderosa pine forests on the outskirts of the town of Sprague River and starts the climb over Switchback Hill. Riding uphill on the loose gravel, even with a 2-percent grade, is exhausting. Standing to pump can cause the back tire to spinout, but you're down to your granny gear if you sit. You can skip the tortuous climb by taking Klamath County Route 1101 to the top of the hill, and turning onto Forest Road 22 to meet the trail for the downhill ride to Squaw Flat. The trail is smoother and more packed between Switchback Hill and Horton. Between Horton and Olene, sections of loose basalt are encountered again. From Squaw Flat to Dairy, the trail passes through desert and pasture. The trail comes within sight of the cafe in Dairy, and crosses to the south side of OR 140 just west of Dairy. The trail remains close to OR 140, crossing it twice between Dairy and Olene. From Olene to the paved section, a finer grade of packed gravel makes riding easier. Traffic on the trail increases as it approaches Klamath Falls.

OC & E Woods Line State Trail: Woods Line Branch

(The information for this ride was provided by Art Svigney, President of the Klamath Falls Rails to Trails Group.)

This section of the state trail, originally the Weyerhaeuser Woods Line, was built in 1940. The trail starts just northeast of Beatty at mile 52 on the OC & E main trail. About 1 mile farther north, you come across the old railroad maintenance yard (Sycan Shops) and the line's old snowplow, #32. The 1941 snowplow kept the Woods Line open in winter. After passing the snowplow, the trail meanders through pine groves as it gradually gains elevation. The first 7 miles consist of loose cinder ballast and are a good workout. However, despite the surface, I had little trouble negotiating the trail. The trail offers great vistas and wildlife viewing.

General location:	Between Beatty and Thompson Reservoir, about 50 miles northeast of Klamath Falls.
Distance:	34 miles (Beatty to Sycan Marsh), 17 miles (Thompson Reservoir to Camp 9 Site), one way.
Time:	10 hours.
Aerobic level:	Easy to strenuous, depending on the length and section traveled.
Elevation change:	The trail ascends 600 feet between Beatty and Sycan Marsh and has a maximum grade of 3 percent. From Thompson Reservoir to Camp 9, the trail climbs 1,300 feet and has a maximum grade of 3 percent.
Tread:	Loose cinders cover most of the route. The cinders are packed on some sections and are easier to ride than the loose basalt on the OC & E Main Line.
Technical difficulty:	3.
Hazards:	The 100-foot-high Merritt Creek Trestle will not be safe to cross until it has decking and railings. Bring plenty of drinking water.
Season:	The trail is open year-round, but it is usually snow-covered from November to May.
Services:	Beatty and Silver Lake offer basic services. All services are available in Klamath Falls. Drinking water is not available along the trail except at the two campgrounds on Thompson Reservoir.
Rescue index:	You may be able to get help at the Camp Six Guard Station, 1.3 miles east of Horse Glade Trailhead; the Puddle Springs Work Center, 2 miles north of Camp 9 in Silver Lake; or in Bly.
Land status:	The trail is a state trail and passes through National Forest and private land. Please respect private property.
Maps:	Call the Oregon State Parks and Recreation Department for a free trail map. Other maps include the Fremont National Forest recreation map; and the Bly, Silver Lake, and Paisley Ranger District maps. USGS: Ponina Butte, Rodeo Butte, River Bed Butte, River Bed Butte Spring, Sycan Marsh West, Sycan Marsh East, Pole Butte, Thompson Reservoir, and Partin Butte.

Sources of additional information: Oregon State Parks and Recreation Department; Collier Memorial State Park; Klamath Rails-to-Trails; Fremont National Forest, Bly Ranger District.

Finding the trail: To reach Sycan Siding Trailhead, take Oregon Highway 140 approximately 36 miles east of Klamath Falls to Beatty. Head 2.1 miles north on Godowa Springs Road, then east on Sycan Road. When the pavement turns to dirt, turn right and follow the road south until you see a big yellow railroad snowplow. You can park near the snowplow. The Woods Line is located behind the plow. The Woods Line intersects the OC & E main line 1 mile to the south. To reach Horse Glade Trailhead, continue

OC & E WOODS LINE STATE TRAIL
WOODS LINE BRANCH

Ride 29

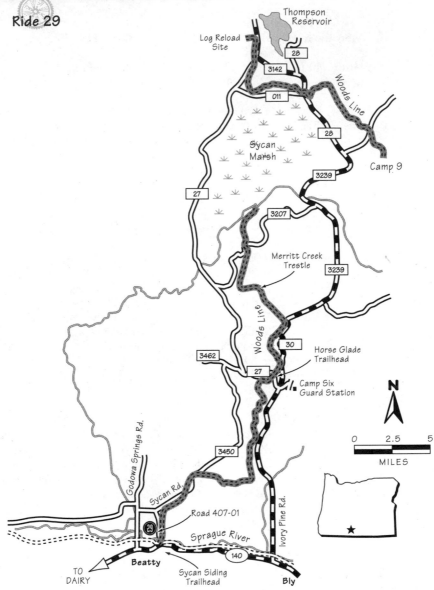

15 miles east of Beatty on OR 140. Turn north on Ivory Pine Road (Forest Road 30) and ride for 12.5 miles. Turn left onto FR 27 (heading toward Thompson Reservoir). The trailhead is about 1.3 miles down FR 27 on the right. The trail may also be accessed from various Forest Service roads.

THE RIDE

Nine miles up the trail from Sycan Siding, there is an old abandoned trestle that is about 400 feet long and more than 100 feet tall. To the east, several hundred feet down, is Five Mile Creek. From this point, the trail is mostly on national forest land, but it also passes through some private property. Keep an eye out for boundary markers if you leave the trail. Farther up the trail, Five Mile Creek crosses under the trail five times. This area has wooded hills on either side. It is a nice place to kick back and relax along the creek. As the trail continues to climb at a 2- to 3-percent grade, the creek stays on the west side and the trail surface varies from loose to relatively packed cinders.

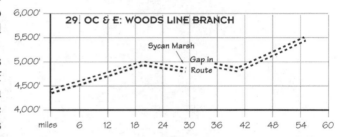

The trail passes through a series of small canyons. You reach Horse Glade Trailhead 19 miles

Sycan Marsh from Sycan Butte.

Beware! Poison oak is found in many areas of Oregon.

from the start, a National Forest facility with a modern vault toilet, but no water. I personally like the southern part of this trail best, but that is not to discount the northern part. The trail passes through various meadows and recent logging operations. Eight miles north of the Horse Glade Trailhead is the 400-foot long Merritt Creek Trestle. The decking on the trestle was not finished in 1997, but the Forest Service plans to complete the decking soon. Without the railings and decking, the trestle is not safe to cross, but you can walk across the creek most of the summer. The trail climbs to Sycan Marsh, but does not continue across the marsh. Most of the marsh is owned by The Nature Conservancy and managed as a wildlife refuge. The trail resumes on the north side of the marsh. Access the trail from Forest Road 011. Just north of FR 011, the trail splits to the north and east. To the east, the trail continues for 12 miles, climbing to 6,100 feet. To the north, the trail proceeds 5 miles to Thompson Reservoir, which has two campgrounds with drinking water. The trail winds and twists as it climbs through tree stands along steep drop-offs. The end of the trail is the log-loading area. The trail is crossed and paralleled by numerous Forest Service roads, which provide multiple loop opportunities.

Central Oregon

From Central Oregon's desert, you can see the icy tops of the Cascades 70 miles away. Hood, Jefferson, Washington, the Three Sisters, Broken-top, Bachelor, Diamond Peak, and Thielsen are the first peaks to appear through the dusty air. As you get closer, you can discern the gentle folds of the forest carpet that leads to the peaks. Many of the best bike trails in the state are on these east-facing slopes of the Cascades. Over many years, the volcanoes have covered the eastern slope with a thick blanket of ash and pumice, which provides a smooth, fast, sandy trail surface. A 1,000-mile network of roads and trails lies beneath the forest canopy, from the juniper and pine forests at the desert's edge, to the firs along the Cascades' crest. Riders soon learn that the slopes which appear so gentle from a distance can also be very steep. This collection of rides begins at Santiam Pass. The pumice plain east of Hoodoo Ski Bowl contains miles of marked cross-country ski and snowmobile trails that are open for biking from May to October. A dozen lakes are scattered along the edge of the plain, and Ride 30 brings riders past most of these lakes on winter recreation trails.

Just below the pass, Suttle and Blue lakes are visible from U.S. Highway 20 and Mount Washington dominates the skyline to the south. Ride 31 circles Suttle Lake and two smaller lakes, Scout and Dark, that are ideal for swimming on a hot day. The Suttle Lake Resort can satisfy your thirst and hunger after your ride, or you can head east to the boardwalks and shops of Sisters. Families will love starting and ending rides in Sisters. The easy Eagle Rock Ride (Ride 32) and the longer Peterson Ridge Ride (Ride 33) start at the Sisters City Park. Ending a ride with a picnic under the sweet-smelling ponderosa pine will invigorate a tired pack of riders.

Turn south from the center of Sisters on the Three Creeks Road to reach two strenuous and technically challenging rides, Rides 34 and 35. These figure-eights offer riders many options for length and difficulty. The Snow Creek Loop is smoother, but the Three Creeks Loop offers grander vistas. Rough roads and bike trails connect the Three Creeks Basin to the Tumalo Creek Basin to the south, but most people get to Tumalo Creek by going through Bend.

Bend is a paradise for people seeking outdoor adventure. Bicyclists are especially fortunate because some trails in Central Oregon are open all year. The weather is great; the skies are clear enough to see the mountains; public lands surround the town, and Bend is large enough to support several good restaurants. Most people who ride mountain bikes also ski, run, hike, raft, climb, and/or camp, and Central Oregon contains opportunities to do all of these.

Bend's drinking water comes from the Tumalo Valley, west of town. The broad ridge between the Tumalo Valley and the Cascade Lakes Highway harbors several trail systems that you can ride to from Bend; these systems are linked to other trail systems north and south along the Cascades. Desert trails start along the eastern edge of Bend. The Swampy Lakes Trail (Ride 36) can be accessed either from Skyliner Road up the Tumalo Valley or the Cascades Lakes Highway. The short trail to 90-foot Tumalo Falls (Ride 37) is a rewarding addition or alternative to the Swampy Lakes Trail. Farther out the Cascade Lakes Highway, the Lava Lake to Sparks Lake Trail (Ride 38) offers a longer, more remote ride that can be extended to a loop around Mt. Bachelor. Closer to town, Phils Loop (Ride 39) can be too much fun; maintain control on your descent or those screams of glee will turn to wails of pain. The spectacular Upper Deschutes River Trail (Ride 40) has become so popular that hikers, bikers, equestrians, and auto-drivers have their own trails. Go on weekdays or at dawn to avoid adding to the congestion. Ride 41, the Lower Deschutes River Trail, starts 170 river miles downstream from Bend where the Deschutes joins the Columbia River. You will see more boaters than trail users on a ride up the canyon. Don't attempt the 32-mile rail-to-trail ride on a mid-summer's day; temperatures can exceed 110 degrees. This ride is best done in the spring to catch the wildflowers and orchards in bloom. The Davis Lake to Bobby Lake Trail (Ride 42) is a summer and fall ride because snow blocks the trail through winter and spring. Davis Lake is one of several large lakes between Mt. Bachelor and Diamond Peak. Most of the lakes are surrounded by bike trails and roads.

Hoodoo to Link Lake Loop

South of U.S. Highway 20 at Santiam Pass, a broad pumice plain is criss-crossed with miles of cross-country ski and snowmobile trails suitable for bicycling. The craggy tops of Three Fingered Jack and Mount Washington set the northern and southern boundaries of this plain. Hayrick Butte and Cache Mountain form the western and eastern boundaries. The trails wind through an old burn covered with young lodgepole pine. This route starts at the Hoodoo Ski Area parking lot and climbs over the pass between Hoodoo and Hayrick buttes before descending to the trails across the plain. The trail drops into fir and hemlock forests east of the plain and passes seven small lakes below Cache Mountain. Each lake has a unique shape and setting. By August, the larger lakes are ideal for swimming. The route returns across the plain to Ray Benson Sno-park and back to the trailhead at Hoodoo.

HOODOO TO LINK LAKE LOOP

Ride 30

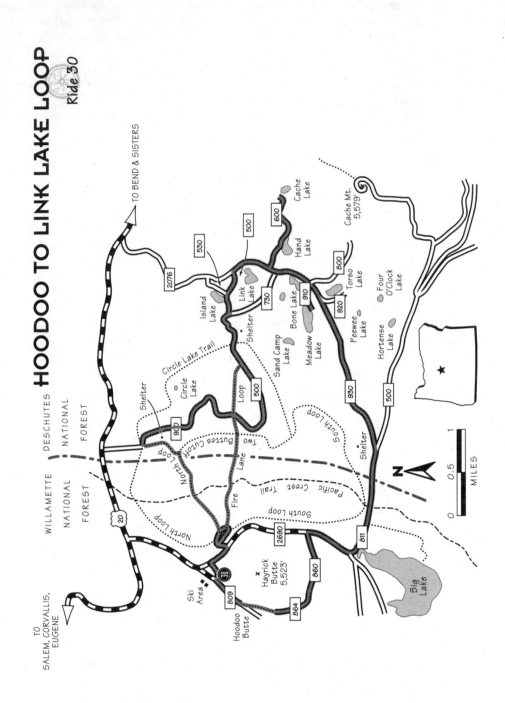

General location:	On Santiam Pass, 30 miles west of Sisters in Central Oregon.
Distance:	14.4 miles, loop.
Time:	2 to 3 hours.
Aerobic level:	Moderate.
Elevation change:	Total elevation gain is 1,600 feet.
Tread:	10.5 miles dirt/gravel roads, 1.2 miles paved road, 2.7 miles singletrack.
Technical difficulty:	Level 3.
Hazards:	The number of trails and roads can be confusing; get the recommended maps. Some of the roads and trails are used by motorcycles and ORVs; stay out of their way.
Season:	The trails are free of snow from June to November. The sandy roads and trails drain quickly. They may also become very soft by late summer.
Services:	Sisters has all services
Rescue index:	Seek help in Sisters.
Land status:	Willamette National Forest, McKenzie Ranger District; Deschutes National Forest, Sisters Ranger District.
Maps:	Sisters Ranger District Map; the Imus Geographics' map of the Santiam Pass Winter Recreation Area is the best map of ski and snowmobile trails, which are good trails to explore. USGS: Mt. Washington and Three Fingered Jack.

Sources of additional information: Willamette and Deschutes National Forests (see Appendix).

Finding the trail: At the top of Santiam Pass, 30 miles west of Sisters, turn south from U.S. Highway 20 onto the road marked for Hoodoo Ski Bowl and Ray Benson Sno-Park. Drive 1.2 miles to the maintenance shed at the Hoodoo Ski Area, at the south end of the large parking lot. The trail between Hoodoo and Hayrick buttes starts here.

THE RIDE

From the south end of the Hoodoo Ski Bowl parking lot, pass by the maintenance shops and head for the pass between Hayrick and Hoodoo buttes. Hayrick is the butte with the basalt cliffs. Hoodoo Butte has a ski lift to the top. A half-mile up the road, a narrow trail leads to the right and follows the bottom of the valley to the pass between the buttes. The trail is used by off-road vehicles and leads from the pass down the west slope of Hayrick Butte to Forest Road 864.

Follow FR 864 for 0.4 mile to FR 860. You should start seeing the orange diamonds that mark the snowmobile trails. The trail follows snowmobile or cross-country skiing trail markers for the rest of the ride, except for the side

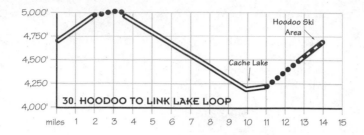

trip to Cache Lake. Turn left (east) on FR 860 and travel 0.7 mile before taking a right turn onto the 2690 (paved). Head south on the pavement for 0.7 mile and turn left on FR 811 (gravel and dirt). Look for Big Lake to the south of FR 811. This is the Historic Santiam Pass Wagon Road. The road numbers change when you leave the Willamette and enter the Deschutes National Forest; FR 811 becomes FR 500. Follow the signs toward Corbett Sno-Park.

This snowmobile trail follows FR 930 for 1.8 miles before it merges with FR 2076—the mainline road to Corbett Sno-Park. About 0.2 mile past the 930/2076 junction are the spur roads to Meadow and Torso lakes—Forest Roads 910 and 920, respectively. Continue on FR 2076 for another 0.5 mile to FR 600. Turn right on 600 for a mile ride to Cache Lake, passing Hand Lake on the way. Return to the 2076/600 junction and ride north for 0.8 mile to FR 500. Turn left onto 500 and pass between Link and Island lakes. If you have time, explore some of the intersecting cross-country ski trails. The blue diamonds mark the ski trails and the signs give directions back to the sno-park. **Important Note: Do not ride on the Pacific Crest Trail.**

Suttle Lake to Dark Lake

Bring your swimsuit for this three-lake tour and plan on having dinner at Suttle Lake Resort after you finish your ride. Situated on the eastern end of the lake, the porch outside the restaurant catches the last rays of summer sun. Winds coming over the pass keep Suttle Lake choppy most of the time. Scout Lake is the smallest and shallowest of the three lakes, so it gets warm sooner. Ride around Scout Lake to find the best swimming hole. I found a rope swing to dive from on the east side of the lake. Dark Lake lies shaded and still in a fir-lined bowl. Diving into this little lake sends ripples to the far shore. I had to ride up to Forest Road 2068 to generate enough heat to warrant a swim in the cool waters of Dark Lake. The trail along the north

SUTTLE LAKE TO DARK LAKE

Ride 31

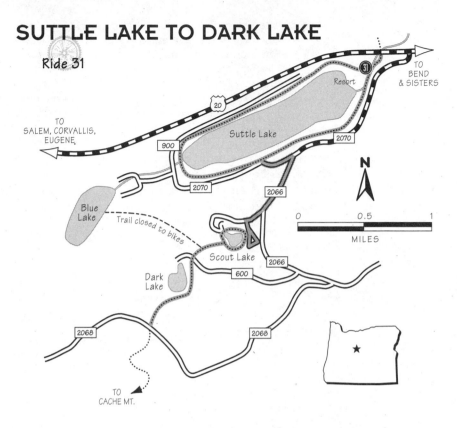

shore of Suttle Lake receives less use than the south shore and offers several isolated swimming spots. More advanced riders may want to add the 2,000-foot climb to the top of Cache Mountain to get enough exercise.

General location:	12 miles west of Sisters.
Distance:	8.2-mile loop, including the out-and-back ride to Dark Lake.
Time:	1 to 2 hours.
Aerobic level:	Moderate.
Elevation change:	The ride around Suttle Lake is nearly flat. The trail climbs 550 feet to reach the road above Dark Lake.
Tread:	This route has 1.6 miles on paved road and 6.6 miles on singletrack.
Technical difficulty:	Level 3.
Hazards:	Be prepared to encounter people on the trails. Trail use has exposed roots along some sections.
Season:	The trail is usually open from May through October.
Services:	Suttle Lake Resort has a small store and cafe. All services are available in Sisters.
Rescue index:	Help may be available at the resort or in Sisters.
Land status:	Deschutes National Forest, Sisters Ranger District.

Maps: The Sisters Ranger District Map provides good
coverage of the area and includes the trail. The Fat
Tire Publications' map, *Mountain Biking Central
Oregon* provides excellent coverage and is water and
tear resistant. Most bike stores carry the Fat Tire
map. The Forest Service also publishes brochures for
mountain biking in Central Oregon. USGS: Three
Fingered Jack, Black Butte.

Sources of additional information: The Forest Service office in Sisters
has additional information about the area.

Finding the trail: Take U.S. Highway 20 west of Sisters for 12 miles. Turn
south on Forest Road 2070 and follow the signs to Suttle Lake Resort.

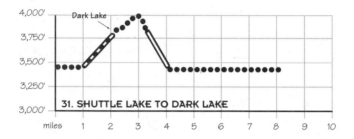

THE RIDE

The trail starts at a footbridge over Lake Creek, southeast of Suttle Lake
Resort. Follow the trail clockwise around the lake. After leaving the resort
area, the trail passes through hardwoods and firs along the shore for 0.5
mile before reaching Blue Bay Campground. South Shore Campground is
about 0.4 mile past Blue Bay Campground. Leave the trail at South Shore
Campground and follow the paved road out of the campground to Forest
Road 2070 (paved). Turn right on FR 2070 and follow it 0.1 mile to its junction with FR 2066. Turn left onto FR 2066 (paved) and follow the signs to
Scout Lake. A trail circles Scout Lake. You can ride it in either direction, but
watch for the signed trail junction on the west side of the lake that leads to
Blue Lake and Dark Lake. Follow the trail west from Scout Lake for 0.4 mile
to where the trail splits. Take the left fork. The right fork leads to private
land and Blue Lake. Dark Lake is only 0.2 mile uphill from this junction.
The trail arrives at a picnic area on the east shore of Dark Lake. Camp
Tamarack (private) is on the opposite shore. The trail skirts the east shore
then climbs at a moderately steep grade for 0.4 mile to FR 2068 (gravel) and
the turnaround point. Retrace your route back to South Shore Campground,
then follow the Suttle Lake Trail the rest of the way around the lake.

Eagle Rock Loop

This nearly flat ride follows the same route as the Peterson Ridge Loop, Ride 33, for its first 3.6 miles. Village Green Park, at the start of the trail, has restrooms and water. The park is a nice place to picnic after a ride. Brown, 3-foot posts mark the route and make the trail easy to follow. The route travels through ponderosa pine and juniper forests. Sage, bitterbrush, manzanita, and ceanothus compose most of the ground vegetation. Riders can catch glimpses of the volcanoes forming the crest of the Cascades. Try this ride in the spring to see wildflowers and more wildlife. This ride is for families and beginners. Late in summer, sections of the tread become soft pumice or sand, making the trip much more strenuous or even impassable.

General location:	The trail starts in Sisters.
Distance:	6.6 miles, out-and-back with a short loop on the end.
Time:	1 hour.
Aerobic level:	Easy.
Elevation change:	The 200-foot gain in elevation is imperceptible.
Tread:	The trail is 4.5 miles of singletrack, 1.5 miles of doubletrack, and 0.6 mile on pavement.
Technical difficulty:	2.
Hazards:	Other trail users are the main hazard. Watch for vehicles when crossing roads.
Season:	Since it is on the edge of the desert, snow seldom closes the trail. By late summer, the trail may become too soft to ride.
Services:	All services are available in Sisters.
Rescue index:	Seek help in Sisters.
Land status:	Deschutes National Forest, Sisters Ranger District.
Maps:	The Sisters Ranger District Map provides good coverage of the area, and includes most of the trail. The Fat Tire Publications map, Mountain Biking Central Oregon, provides excellent coverage and is water and tear resistant. Most bike stores carry this map. The Forest Service also publishes brochures for mountain biking in Central Oregon. USGS: Sisters.

Sources of additional information: The FalconGuide *Mountain Biking Bend* (Helena, MT: Falcon, 1998) gives very detailed descriptions of this ride and thirty others in the Bend area.

Finding the trail: From U.S. Highway 20 in Sisters, turn south on the Three Creek Road near the center of town and go two blocks to the Village Green City Park to park.

EAGLE ROCK
LOOP

Ride 32

PETERSON
RIDGE LOOP

Ride 33

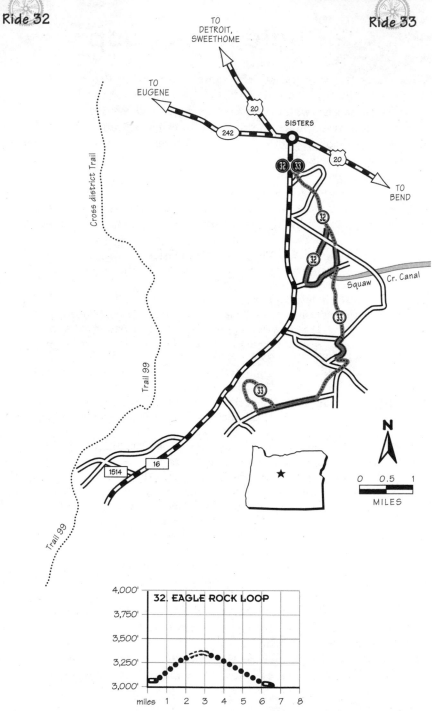

TO
DETROIT,
SWEETHOME

TO
EUGENE

20

242

SISTERS

20

32 33

TO
BEND

32

Cross district Trail

32

Squaw Cr. Canal

33

Trail 99

33

N

1514   16

0   0.5   1

MILES

Trail 99

32. EAGLE ROCK LOOP

4,000'

3,750'

3,500'

3,250'

3,000'

miles 1 2 3 4 5 6 7 8

From the park in Sisters, follow the paved Three Creeks Road (Forest Road 16) 0.3 mile south to the edge of town. The trail leaves the paved road at Tyee Road. Watch for the trail signs on the left side of FR 16. The trail crosses several roads,but the road crossings are well marked. About 2 miles from the trailhead, the trail crosses a small bridge and then splits. This is the start of the loop for the Eagle Rock Trail. Take a right on the doubletrack. The trail follows the doubletrack for 1 mile, until it reaches Squaw Creek Canal, where it follows the canal downstream for about 0.5 mile to a bridge over the canal. A right turn over the bridge leads to the Peterson Ridge Trail. Turn left and head back to Sisters.

See Map
on Page 124

Peterson Ridge Loop

Its start in the picturesque town of Sisters gives this trail bonus points even before you've ridden it. The extensive use of signs makes this trail easy to follow. The trail rolls through ponderosa pine and juniper forests to Peterson Ridge. From Peterson Ridge, riders look to the west across miles of forest to snow-capped volcanic peaks and to the east, over the nearly flat expanse of desert. The scent of pine, sage, and ceanothus perfumes the air. Gray clumps of bitterbrush, a favorite food of deer, are scattered along the trail. Bitterbrush resembles sage but is not as aromatic. Close inspection of a bitterbrush clump will usually reveal nibbled stems.

The Forest Service has burned the underbrush along portions of the trail to try to mimic the natural fire regimen of this ecosystem. Prior to 1800, low intensity fires burned through this area every five to twenty-five years. Controlled burns stimulate plant growth and usually avoid killing the larger trees. More intense fires burned the area along Peterson Ridge and in this area forest recovery is slow. The trail crosses several irrigation ditches that may contain water, depending on the season. The pumice surface of the trail may become impassably soft by late summer.

The ride has enough length and elevation gain to be moderately strenuous. Late in summer, sections of the tread become soft pumice and sand, making the trip much more strenuous. Beginning riders in good condition may find this a good transition to the intermediate technical riding level.

Taking a break on the Peterson Ridge Trail.

General location:	The trail starts in Sisters.
Distance:	17 miles, out and back with a loop on the end.
Time:	1 to 2 hours.
Aerobic level:	Moderate.
Elevation change:	The highest point on the trail, Petersen Ridge, is 700 feet above the trailhead.
Tread:	12.5 miles of singletrack, 3.9 miles of doubletrack, and 0.6 mile on pavement.
Technical difficulty:	3.
Hazards:	Other trail users are the main hazard.
Season:	The trail is seldom closed by snow; it is on the edge of the desert. By late-summer the trail may become too soft to ride.
Services:	All services are available in Sisters.
Rescue index:	Seek help in Sisters.
Land status:	Deschutes National Forest, Sisters Ranger District.
Maps:	The Sisters Ranger District Map provides good coverage of the area, and includes most of the trail. The Fat Tire Publications' map, Mountain Biking Central Oregon, provides excellent coverage and is water and tear resistant. Most bike stores carry the Fat Tire map. The Forest Service also publishes brochures for mountain biking in Central Oregon. USGS: Sisters, Three Creek Butte.

Sources of additional information: The Falconguide *Mountain Biking Bend* (Helena, MT: Falcon, 1998) gives very detailed descriptions of this ride and thirty others in the Bend area.

Finding the trail: From U.S. Highway 20 in Sisters, turn south on the Three Creek Road near the center of town and go two blocks to the Village Green City Park to park.

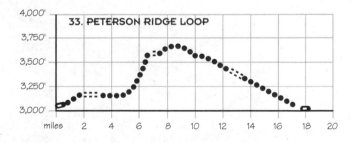

THE RIDE

From the park, follow paved Three Creeks Road (Forest Road 16) south to the edge of town. The trail leaves the paved road at Tyee Road. Watch for the trail signs on the left side of FR 16. Follow the brown trail signs 3.6 miles to the Squaw Creek Canal. The road crossings are well marked, but watch for traffic on the roads. A left turn over the bridge leads to the long loop. The short loop back to Sisters follows the doubletrack along the canal for 0.25 mile before turning toward Sisters. The trail begins the climb up Peterson Ridge after crossing the canal and then levels out after about 2 miles. The ride around the top of the ridge provides good views of the mountains and desert, but you will need to walk to the top of one of the lava promontories to get the best views. On the ride back to Sisters, take a left after crossing the Squaw Creek Canal to do an extra loop.

Snow Creek Loop

This route offers the complete package of physically demanding climbs, technical riding challenges, thrilling descents, biological diversity, and spectacular scenery. The trail follows a cross-country ski route toward the Three Creeks Lake basin. Tam McArthur Rim rises 1,000 feet above the basin and remains snow-covered late into the summer. The trail climbs for 5 miles through lodgepole pine forests that have been thinned by chainsaws and mountain pine beetle. Pine beetle larvae etch web-like patterns on the boles

Passed by kids on BMX bikes—how embarassing!

of trees just under the bark. Thousands of acres of lodgepole in Central Oregon have been killed by the beetles over the past 20 years. The trail turns west before reaching the lake, but some riders may want to take the 2-mile side trip to the lake. The Snow Creek Loop passes through a lunar landscape of pumice reportedly used to train astronauts. The singletrack portion has interesting technical challenges including rocky sections, steep drops, steep ascents, narrow tread, and switchbacks. When the trail descends along Snow Creek, it winds through forests of white fir, Douglas-fir, lodgepole, and ponderosa pine. Many of the largest pines have been cut, but the stands still retain some old growth. The trail crosses several small meadows on its way back to the trailhead. This is the first half of the Three Creek Long Loop (Ride 35).

General location:	10 miles south of Sisters.
Distance:	12.9 miles, loop.
Time:	1 to 2 hours.
Aerobic level:	Moderate.
Elevation change:	From the trailhead at 5,200 feet, the route climbs to 6,300 feet in the first 5 miles, then levels off for about 1.5 miles before descending to the trailhead.
Tread:	3.1 miles of singletrack, 6.5 miles of doubletrack, 3 miles of gravel road, and 0.3 mile of paved road.
Technical difficulty:	4 on singletrack and 2 on other surfaces.
Hazards:	The trail is popular with equestrians. Please give equestrians plenty of warning as you approach and always yield the trail. Equestrian clubs invest thousands of volunteer hours maintaining the trails that you ride.
Season:	Snow keeps this trail closed until July most years and blocks the trail again by mid-October.
Services:	All services are available in Sisters.
Rescue index:	Seek help in Sisters.
Land status:	Deschutes National Forest, Sisters Ranger District.
Maps:	The Sisters Ranger District Map provides good coverage of the area, and includes the trail. The Fat Tire Publications' map, Mountain Biking Central Oregon, provides excellent coverage and is water and tear resistant. Most bike stores carry the Fat Tire map. The Forest Service also publishes brochures for mountain biking in Central Oregon. USGS: Tumalo Falls, Broken Top, Three Creek Butte, Trout Creek Butte.

Sources of additional information: The FalconGuide *Mountain Biking Bend* (Helena, MT: Falcon, 1998) gives very detailed descriptions of this ride and thirty others in the Bend area.

Finding the trail: From Oregon Highway 22 in Sisters, turn south on the paved Three Creek Road (Forest Road 16) near the center of town and drive 10 miles to the Upper Three Creeks Lake Sno-park on the left (east) side of the road.

SNOW CREEK LOOP

Ride 34

THREE CREEKS LONG LOOP

Ride 35

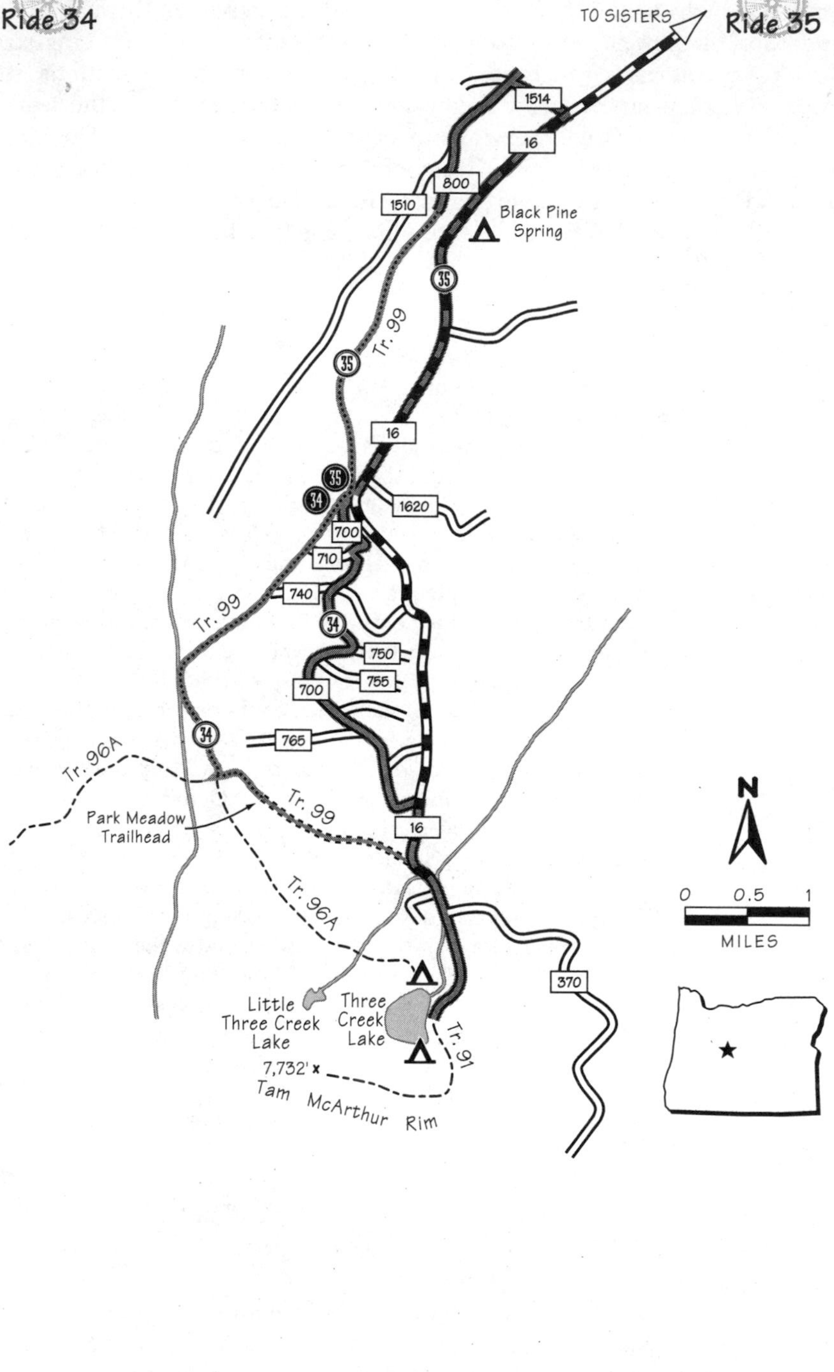

TO SISTERS

1514

16

800

1510

Black Pine Spring

35

Tr. 99

35

16

35

34

1620

700

710

740

34

750

755

700

765

34

Tr. 96A

Tr. 99

Park Meadow
Trailhead

Tr. 96A

16

370

Tr. 99

N

0   0.5   1

MILES

Little
Three Creek
Lake

Three
Creek
Lake

Tr. 91

7,732' ×

Tam McArthur Rim

Follow the paved Three Creeks Road (Forest Road 16) south a few hundred yards to FR 700. This loop follows a cross-country ski trail marked with blue diamonds. Stay on FR 700 for 4.6 miles, until it reaches FR 16; several roads inter-

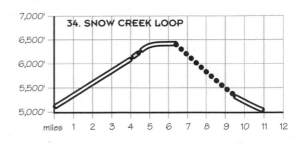

sect FR 700 along the way, but the route uphill is obvious. About 2 miles up FR 700, there is a cross-country ski shelter on the right. Check out the views of Mt. Jefferson from the shelter. When you reach the junction with FR 16 (paved), turn right. The pavement ends after a few hundred yards and turns to gravel. About a 0.5 mile up FR 16, turn right at the sign pointing toward Park Meadow Trailhead; or, continue straight to Three Creek Lake, and then return to the sign.

From the sign, the doubletrack road leads west for 1.5 miles and crosses a large pumice desert before reaching the singletrack. After 0.5 mile, the trail forks. The left fork leads into the Three Sisters Wilderness, where no bikes are allowed. Take the right fork and continue the descent along Snow Creek. Two miles from the junction of trails 96A and 99, Nancy's Ski Trail loop cuts off to the right. Stay to the left. About 0.3 mile past Nancy's cutoff, Warren's ski trail cutoff is to the right. Stay to the left again for 0.8 mile to the last ski trail signs that point to the trailhead. Follow the doubletrack back to FR 700 and the Three Creeks Sno-park. Ride 35 heads north where the blue diamonds end and the yellow diamonds begin.

See Map
on Page 130

Three Creeks Long Loop

So you've done Peterson Ridge, and found it fun but not exhausting. You want a more demanding ride. A serious challenge where families fear to tread. See if you're still grinning after this one. The first half follows the route of Snow Creek Loop, Ride 34. That part has its challenges, but you're still smiling. The second part begins with some steep climbs to an open ridgeline. The clearcuts leave unobstructed views of the Three Sisters, the spire of Mt. Washington, and Mt. Jefferson. They also bear evidence to past over-optimism by the Forest Service. The clearcuts appear to be more than 20 years old and they are still more brushfield than forest. Manzanita and ceanothus line the trail, forcing you to negotiate through the loose rocks. The long descent on the ridgeline will strain your forearms and make the run down the doubletrack a welcome relief. What you may not notice until the ride back up Forest Road 16 is that the descent also gave your quads a workout.

The climb on FR 16 passes above the open pine stands that surround Black Pine Springs and campground. The large yellow-bellied pine with pinegrass groundcover is typical of old-growth ponderosa. This type of forest once covered the east slope of the Cascades from the Yakima Valley in Washington to California. The Forest Service has reversed its policy and is now trying harder to restore this type of forest rather then clearcut it.

General location:	10 miles south of Sisters.
Distance:	19.5 miles, loop.
Time:	3 to 4 hours.
Aerobic level:	Strenuous.
Elevation change:	From the trailhead at 5,200 feet, the route climbs to 6,300 feet in its first 5 miles; it then levels off for about 1.5 miles before descending to the half-way point near the trailhead. The trail then traverses across a slope before descending a long, rocky ridge. A steady climb of 1,000 feet on pavement, back to the trailhead, ends the ride.
Tread:	The trail covers 7.6 miles on singletrack, 6.3 miles on doubletrack, 1.8 miles of gravel road, and 3.8 miles of paved road.
Technical difficulty:	4 on singletrack.
Hazards:	Trail 99 is popular with equestrians. Please give equestrians plenty of warning as you approach and yield the trail if necessary. Equestrian clubs invest thousands of volunteer hours maintaining the trails that you ride.
Season:	Snow keeps this trail closed until July most years and blocks the trail again by mid-October.
Services:	All services are available in Sisters.
Rescue index:	Seek help in Sisters.
Land status:	Deschutes National Forest, Sisters Ranger District.
Maps:	The Sisters Ranger District Map provides good coverage of the area, and includes the trail. The Fat Tire Publications' map, Mountain Biking Central Oregon, provides excellent coverage and is water and tear resistant. Most bike stores carry the Fat Tire map. The Forest Service also publishes brochures for mountain biking in Central Oregon. USGS: Tumalo Falls, Broken Top, Three Creek Butte, Trout Creek Butte.

Sources of additional information: The FalconGuide *Mountain Biking Bend* (Helena, MT: Falcon, 1998) gives very detailed descriptions of this ride and thirty others in the Bend area. This ride is called "Trail 99/Forest Road 700: Long Loop" in the guide.

Finding the trail: From U.S. Highway 2 in Sisters, turn south on the paved Three Creek Road (Forest Road 16) near the center of town and drive 10 miles to the Upper Three Creeks Lake Sno-park on the left (east) side of the road.

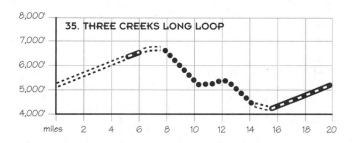

THE RIDE

Follow the directions for Ride 34 to the point where the ride cuts back to the trailhead (about 0.8 mile past Warren's Ski Trail cutoff). Time to decide if you want to continue. The long loop heads to the left and follows the yellow diamonds. The next 4 miles of bruising singletrack offer spectacular views but the loose rock will keep you focused on the trail. After descending the clearcut ridge, you will be pleased to run onto a doubletrack that leads to Forest Road 1510 (gravel). Turn right on FR 1510, ride 0.8 mile, and turn right on FR 1514. Follow FR 1514 back to paved FR 16 and turn right for the long climb back to the Three Creeks Lake Sno-park.

Swampy Lakes Loop

The Swampy Lakes Trail System provides a range of loop options so diverse that families and advanced riders alike will find suitable rides. The northern half of the trail system offers steeper terrain and narrower trails with more roots and rocks than the southern half. The southern half has broad, sandy paths that may get soft in late summer. Beginning riders or those wanting an easier ride should try riding the loops near Swampy Lakes Sno-park.

Most of the trails follow cross-country ski trails marked with blue diamonds; this makes the routes easier to follow. The loop passes three rustic shelters.

The trail system is on an east-west ridge between Skyliner Road and the Cascade Lakes Highway. In 1979, the Bridge Creek Fire burned much of the Tumalo Valley and the trail runs through a portion of the deforested landscape. Riding the loop clockwise avoids the steep ascent of the segment of trail north of Swampy Lakes Shelter. The rocky surface of that section of trail makes descents difficult and limits ascents to those with advanced riding skills. The trail offers splendid views of snow-capped mountains and the Tumalo Valley. It passes through lodgepole pine, ponderosa pine, and Douglas-fir forests. Some areas have been clearcut, some are thinned, and a few are old growth. Early summer is the best season for viewing wildlife.

General location:	The Swampy Lakes trail system is about 15 miles east of Bend.
Distance:	16.6 miles, loop.
Time:	2 to 3 hours.
Aerobic level:	Moderate.
Elevation change:	Riding from Skyliner Road over Swede Ridge to the Cascade Lakes Highway and back includes about 1,600 feet of elevation gain.
Tread:	About 3 miles of the loop are on dirt roads. The rest of the route is well-maintained singletrack.
Technical difficulty:	3.
Hazards:	Trails close to Bend receive moderate-to-heavy use during summer, especially on weekends. Control your speed on the steep descent north of Swampy Lakes shelter. The trail has many exposed roots and rocks.
Season:	Snow usually confines the riding season to June through October.
Services:	All services are available in Bend.
Rescue index:	Seek help in Bend.
Land status:	Deschutes National Forest, Bend Ranger District.
Maps:	The Bend Ranger District Map provides good coverage of the area. The Fat Tire Publications' map, Mountain Biking Central Oregon, provides excellent coverage and is water and tear resistant. Most bike stores carry the Fat Tire map. The Forest Service also publishes brochures with maps about mountain biking in Central Oregon. USGS: Tumalo Falls, Wanoga Butte.

Sources of additional information: In Bend, several bike shops line the roads leading to Skyliner Road and the Cascade Lakes Highway. Many of the personnel in the shops are avid mountain bikers. The FalconGuide *Mountain Biking Bend* (Helena, MT: Falcon, 1998) gives very detailed descriptions of this ride and thirty others in the Bend area.

SWAMPY LAKES LOOP

Ride 36

TUMALO FALLS

Ride 37

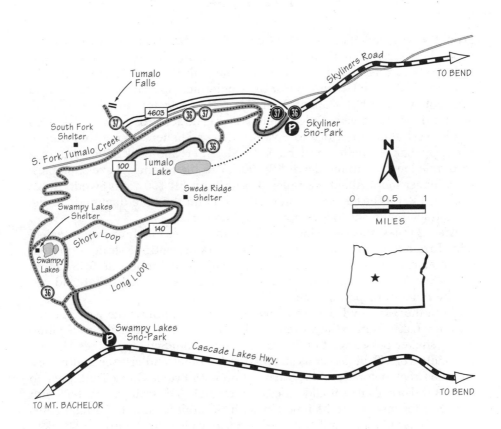

Tumalo Falls

Skyliners Road

TO BEND

4603

37

36 37

37 36

Skyliner Sno-Park

P

South Fork Shelter

37

S. Fork Tumalo Creek

36

100

Tumalo Lake

Swede Ridge Shelter

Swampy Lakes Shelter

Short Loop

140

Long Loop

Swampy Lakes

36

Swampy Lakes Sno-Park

P

Cascade Lakes Hwy.

TO BEND

TO MT. BACHELOR

N

0   0.5   1

MILES

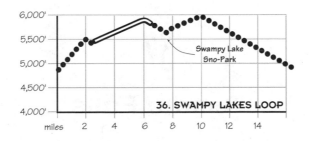

6,000'

5,500'

5,000'

4,500'

4,000'

Swampy Lake Sno-Park

miles   2   4   6   8   10   12   14

36. SWAMPY LAKES LOOP

Finding the trail: The Skyliner Sno-park is 10 miles from Bend. From downtown Bend, take Franklin Avenue west. Franklin becomes Galveston. Keep heading west on Galveston. This street becomes Skyliner Road after leaving Bend.

THE RIDE

From the west end of the Skyliner Sno-park Parking Area, follow the trail as it parallels a gravel road and passes the Oregon Museum of Science and Industry's summer camp. At the junction with the trail to Tumalo Falls, mile point 0.7, turn left and follow the singletrack up a ridge to Forest Road 100. Follow FR 100 for about 2.5 miles to the ridgetop and Swede Ridge Shelter. From the Swede Ridge Shelter, a singletrack/cross-country ski trail heads west along the ridge to Swampy Lakes Shelter. Taking this trail to Swampy Lakes Shelter and back to Skyliner Sno-park gives riders a 13.6-mile loop. Continue down FR 100 for to the Swampy Lakes Sno-park for a longer loop. About 0.8 miles downhill on FR 100 from Swede Ridge Shelter, FR 140 heads west. Follow FR 140 and the blue diamonds to the singletrack that leads to Swampy Lakes Sno-park.

After 2 miles, this easy singletrack section comes to a four-way intersection. Turn left toward Swampy Lakes Sno-park or continue straight through the intersection to cut 2 miles from the loop. The 1-mile ride to Swampy Lakes Sno-park is fast if the road is firm. Watch for the signs that lead you off the road to the parking area.

From the Swampy Lakes Sno-park parking area, follow the well-marked Swampy Lakes Trail to the Swampy Lakes Shelter. The gradual 2-mile climb to the shelter passes west of Swampy Lakes. From Swampy Lakes Shelter, the South Fork Trail descends steeply for 1.5 miles and crosses South Fork Tumalo Creek before reaching the junction with Bridge Creek Trail. Keep to the South Fork Trail as it glides beside the creek. The trail passes the South Fork Shelter just before its junction with the trail leading to Tumalo Falls. Turn right (east) for a 3-mile ride through the Bridge Creek burn and back to the Skyliner Trailhead.

See Map
on Page 135

Tumalo Falls

In 1979, much of the Tumalo Valley burned. This trail traverses the southern edge of the burn and overlooks the deforested valley. Honey-scented ceonothus brushfields cover large areas and border the trail. Fires stimulate ceonothus regeneration and ceonothus adds nitrogen to soils. Ceonothus will also scratch harsh lessons on riders who become too distracted by the scenery. Lodgepole and ponderosa pine are beginning to appear above the brush on north aspects and the valley bottom, but the parched southern exposure may remain brush-covered for decades. The 90-foot falls is visible from the trail for miles. The Tumalo watershed provides Bend's drinking water. This trail is too short for much of a workout, but it is a moderately challenging ride.

General location:	10 miles west of Bend.
Distance:	7.6 miles, out and back.
Time:	1 to 2 hours.
Aerobic level:	Easy.
Elevation change:	The rolling grade provides about 600 feet of climbing.
Tread:	Singletrack.
Technical difficulty:	3.
Hazards:	The downhill edge of the trail collapsed in places and inattentive riders may be pitched into the brush.
Season:	The trail is open from late May through October.
Services:	All services are available in Bend.
Rescue index:	Seek help in Bend.
Land status:	Deschutes National Forest, Bend Ranger District. The Skyliner Sno-park is now managed by Deschutes County.
Maps:	The Bend Ranger District Map provides good coverage of the area. The Fat Tire Publications' map, Mountain Biking Central Oregon, provides excellent coverage and is water and tear resistant. Most bike stores carry the Fat Tire map. The Forest Service also publishes brochures about mountain biking in Central Oregon. USGS: Tumalo Falls.

Sources of additional information: In Bend, several bike shops line the roads leading to Skyliner Road and the Cascade Lakes Highway. Many of the personnel in the shops are avid mountain bikers willing to share trail information. The FalconGuide *Mountain Biking Bend* (Helena, MT: Falcon, 1998) gives very detailed descriptions of this ride and thirty others in the Bend area.

Finding the trail: The trailhead at Skyliner Sno-park, is 10 miles from Bend. From downtown Bend, take Franklin Avenue west. Franklin becomes Galveston. Keep heading west on Galveston. This street becomes Skyliner Road after leaving Bend.

THE RIDE

From the west end of the Skyliner Sno-park Parking Area, follow the trail as it parallels a gravel road and passes the Oregon Museum of Science and

Industry's summer camp. At the junction with the trail to Swede Ridge, mile point 0.7, take the right fork to Tumalo Falls. (The trail to Swede Ridge is part of the Swampy Lakes Loop, Ride 36.) About 0.5 mile farther up the trail, a trail leads left to the OMSI summer camp. Stay on the Tumalo Falls Trail. Just past the South Fork Tumalo Creek crossing, the South Fork Trail comes in from the left. The South Fork Shelter is about 0.5 mile up this trail. Continue on the Tumalo Falls Trail for 2 miles to the Tumalo Falls Picnic Area and Overlook. Park your bike at the overlook—bikes are not allowed on the last 0.5 mile of trail to the base of Tumalo Falls. You may take Forest Road 4603 back to the trailhead or return on the trail. The gravel road has auto traffic and is very dusty by mid-summer.

38

Lava Lake to Sparks Lake: Trails 4 and 99

This classic trip gives riders snow-capped mountain views, crystal-clear lakes for swimming, and a full day of technical riding challenges on singletrack. The trail winds through a maze of recent lava flows between Hosmer and Lava lakes. Most of the forest is lodgepole pine with some spruce and fir. Starting at Lava Lake saves the longest descents for the second half of the ride. The side trail to Quinn Meadows lets riders choose shorter loops. If 22 miles of singletrack are too intimidating, try riding the 16-mile loop from Lava Lake to Quinn Meadows on the highway, then down the trail back to Lava Lake. The 13-mile loop from Quinn Meadows to Sparks Lake on the highway, and back to Quinn Meadows on the trail, is an easy ride with few technical challenges. The trail receives surprisingly heavy use in spite of its remoteness. Watch for equestrians.

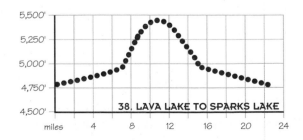

LAVA LAKE TO SPARKS LAKE

Ride 38

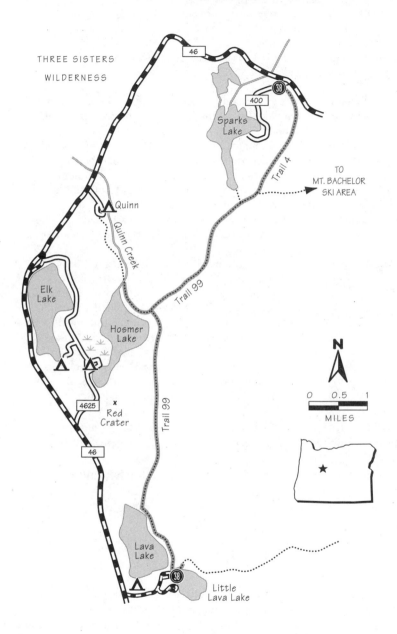

THREE SISTERS
WILDERNESS

46

Sparks
Lake

400   38

Trail 4

TO
MT. BACHELOR
SKI AREA

Quinn

Quinn Creek

Trail 99

Elk
Lake

Hosmer
Lake

4625

Red
Crater

Trail 99

46

N

0   0.5   1

MILES

Lava
Lake

38

Little
Lava Lake

General location:	The trail is on the west side of Mt. Bachelor, 30 miles west of Bend.
Distance:	22.6 miles, out and back.
Time:	3 to 4 hours.
Aerobic level:	Moderate.
Elevation change:	Sparks Lake is 700 feet higher than Lava Lake.
Tread:	Singletrack.
Technical difficulty:	3.
Season:	The trail is usually open from June to mid-October.
Services:	Lava Lake has a small store. All services are available in Bend.
Hazards:	This remote trail requires that you come prepared for wilderness travel and sudden weather changes, with adequate food, clothing, bike repair equipment, and water to complete the trip. Rock outcrops and loose rock on the trail are common.
Rescue index:	The store on the south shore of Lava Lake is open in the summer and has a phone, or you can seek help in Bend.
Land status:	Deschutes National Forest, Bend Ranger District.
Maps:	The Bend Ranger District Map provides good coverage of the area, but does not show the trail. The Deschutes National Forest map shows the trail. The Fat Tire Publications' map, Mountain Biking Central Oregon, provides excellent coverage and is water and tear resistant. Most bike stores carry the Fat Tire map. The Forest Service also publishes brochures for mountain biking in Central Oregon. USGS: Broken Top, South Sister, Elk Lake, Bachelor Butte.

Sources of additional information: The FalconGuide *Mountain Biking Bend* (Helena, MT: Falcon, 1998) gives very detailed descriptions of this ride and thirty others in the Bend area.

Finding the trail: Take the Cascades Lakes Highway (which eventually turns into Forest Road 46) from Bend to the Sparks Lake or Lava Lake trailheads. The trailheads are 26 miles and 39 miles from Bend, respectively.

THE RIDE

From the Lava Lake Trailhead at the far east end of Lava Lake Campground, follow the trail north along the east shore of Lava Lake. Stay to the left at the junction with the Edison/Little Lava Lake Trail, which is a few hundred yards from the trailhead. The 1.5-mile traverse along the lakeshore is challenging. The trail leaves the north end of the lake and climbs gradually through lava flows and lodgepole pines for nearly 4 miles before meeting the junction with Quinn Meadow Trail.

If you follow the Quinn Meadows Trail for 0.5 mile, you come to a bluff overlooking Hosmer Lake. Keep to the right at the trail junction to get to Sparks Lake. About 2.5 miles from the Quinn Meadows Trail junction, you get a glimpse of Sparks Lake. Shortly after you first see the lake, you pass a short, steep trail to the left that leads to a cove on the south shore of Sparks Lake. South Sister provides a stunning backdrop for this quiet picnic site on the cove.

Climb back to the Sparks Lake Trail. About 0.4 mile from this side trail, the Sparks Lake Trail (Trail 4) forks to the left when it meets the trail coming from Mt. Bachelor Ski Area. From here, the Sparks Lake Trailhead on the Cascades Lakes Highway is 3 miles away, over moderately easy terrain. The return trip can be made on the trail or on the highway. The highway is faster, but about 3 miles longer.

Phil's Trail, #24.5

This is a trail for people who ride for the pleasure of riding. Its only expansive views are from the hilltop at the west end. The historic highlights are limited to the piles of rusty cans left by loggers. The forest is a uniform expanse of small-diameter ponderosa pine. Yet, this is one of the most popular rides in Oregon because it is so much fun. The trail has one of the longest and smoothest downhill singletrack runs in the state, and the brown trail posts make the trail easy to follow. Staying on the trail through the downhill curves provides an exhilarating challenge. The difficult rocky sections are confined to the initial descent from the western hilltop and the drop through a canyon along rimrock. Another reason this trail is so popular is that you can start the ride from downtown Bend.

General location:	2.5 miles west of Bend.
Distance:	13.3 miles, loop.
Time:	1 to 2 hours.
Aerobic level:	Moderate.
Hazards:	The rocky area below the summit, on the west end of the trail, is difficult but short. Numerous roads cross the trail, but most crossings are signed.
Elevation change:	This loop has 1,200 feet of elevation gain.
Tread:	This loop has 8.9 miles of singletrack and 4.4 miles of doubletrack/roads.
Technical difficulty:	3.
Season:	The snow-free season is usually May through October.

PHIL'S TRAIL #24.5

Ride 39

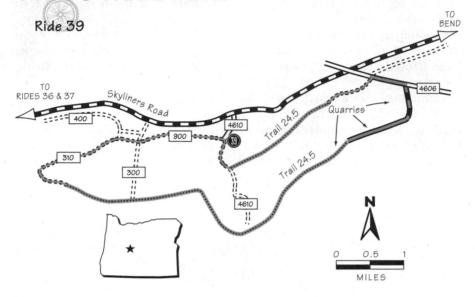

Services:	All services are available in Bend.
Rescue index:	Seek help in Bend.
Land status:	Deschutes National Forest, Bend Ranger District.
Maps:	The Bend Ranger District Map provides good coverage of the area, but does not show the trail. The Fat Tire Publications' map, Mountain Biking Central Oregon, provides excellent coverage and is water and tear resistant. Most bike stores carry the Fat Tire map. The Forest Service also publishes brochures about mountain biking in Central Oregon. USGS: Bend and Tumald falls.

Sources of additional information: The FalconGuide *Mountain Biking Bend* (Helena, MT: Falcon, 1998) gives very detailed descriptions of this ride and thirty others in the Bend area.

Finding the trail: Several roads that head south from Skyliner Road intersect the trail. From downtown Bend, take Franklin Avenue west. Franklin becomes Galveston. Keep heading west on Galveston. This street becomes Skyliners Road after leaving Bend. The first trailhead is on Forest Road 220

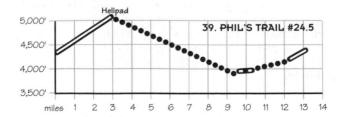

(paved), 2.5 miles from Bend. The trail starts at the junction of Forest Roads 220 and 4606. FR 4610 is 5.5 miles from Bend and the trailhead is at the junction of Forest Roads 4610 and 900. FR 300 is 7 miles from Bend, and the trailhead is at the junction with FR 310.

THE RIDE

If you start riding at the junction of Forest Roads 4610 and 900, you split the uphill segment in half—half at the beginning and half at the end of the ride. Breaking up the climb makes this an easy ride. Start the ride in Bend if you want a better workout. Starting at the junction of Forest Roads 900 and 4610, follow FR 900 1.7 miles west to FR 300. (A singletrack is developing that parallels FR 900 and starts just north of its junction with FR 4610. The singletrack crosses back and forth across the road until it ends on FR 300).

You cross Forest Roads 290 and 364 before getting to FR 300. Across FR 300 is Forest Road 310. Follow FR 310, watching for the brown trail marker on the left that is the start of the singletrack. The singletrack climbs over the hill and through a thicket of manzanita before starting a steep descent. If you care for your health and your bike you will walk part of the downhill through the boulders. The next 6 miles descend on well-marked singletrack. About 1.5 miles after crossing the cinder-covered FR 300, the trail splits. Take the right fork. The trail continues to descend. Watch for the trail signs and follow the bike tracks at the road crossings. The trail drops into a canyon and emerges below rimrock.

Follow an old doubletrack for a short distance along the base of rimrock, until it runs onto a white cinder road. Follow the road past the cinder pit, gate, and trailhead to a paved road, FR 220. Follow FR 220 north 0.5 mile to FR 4606 (gravel) and turn left. Trail signs mark the 2-mile trip back to FR 4610. When you reach the heavily used FR 4610, turn right and ride 0.5 mile back to the trailhead.

Deschutes River Trail: Lava Island to Benham Falls

The Deschutes River Trail has become so popular that hikers, cars, equestrians, and cyclists have their own trails. The bike trail is a mix of singletrack and roads. Most of the roads are closed to motorized vehicles. Trail use is

DESCHUTES RIVER TRAIL
LAVA ISLAND: BENHAM FALLS

Ride 40

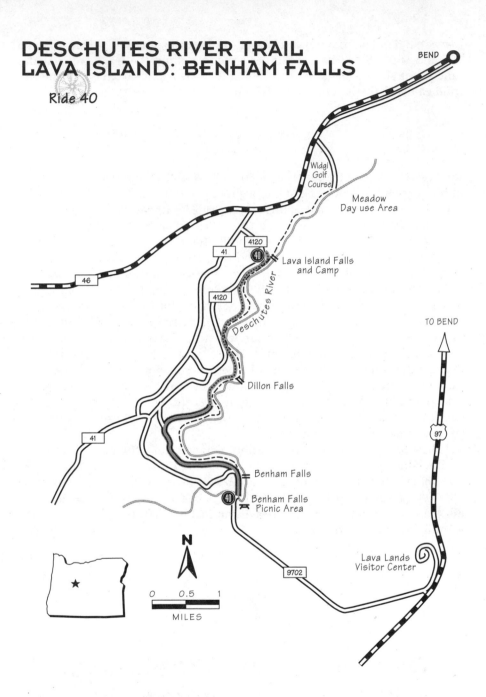

BEND

Widgi Golf Course

Meadow Day use Area

4120

41

40

Lava Island Falls and Camp

46

4120

Deschutes River

Dillon Falls

41

TO BEND

97

Benham Falls

40

Benham Falls Picnic Area

N

Lava Lands Visitor Center

9702

0   0.5   1
MILES

heaviest on weekends. This is not a trail for those wanting to go fast. The heavy traffic and scenery require a leisurely pace. This route starts at Lava Island. A recent lava flow channeled this section of the Deschutes and created several falls. Glassy pools and marshes fill the stretches between the falls. You can start this ride from Lava Island near the Inn at the Seventh Mountain or from the Benham Falls Picnic Area, off U.S. Highway 97. Starting in Bend adds 17 miles to the ride, if you're so inclined.

General location:	The trailhead at Lava Island is about 10 miles south of Bend.
Distance:	13.8 miles, out and back.
Time:	2 hours.
Aerobic level:	Easy.
Elevation change:	The trail has many minor dips and climbs, but is generally flat.
Tread:	Singletrack and dirt road, well-maintained.
Technical difficulty:	3.
Hazards:	The heavy traffic on the trail necessitates that riders proceed cautiously. If the traffic on the trail becomes unbearable, try riding the roads that parallel the trail. The trail hugs several cliffs above the Deschutes River.
Season:	Heavy traffic discourages use during holidays and summer weekends. The trail may be open year-round when winters are mild.
Services:	All services are available in Bend.
Rescue index:	Seek help in Bend.
Land status:	Deschutes National Forest, Bend Ranger District.
Maps:	The Bend Ranger District Map provides good coverage. The Fat Tire Publications' map, Mountain Biking Central Oregon, provides excellent coverage and is water and tear resistant. Most bike stores carry the Fat Tire map. The Forest Service also publishes individual trail information sheets and a brochure about mountain biking in Central Oregon. USGS: Bend, Shevlin Park, Lava Butte, Benham Falls.

Sources of additional information: The Bend Ranger District Map provides good coverage of the area, but does not include all the trails. The FalconGuide, *Mountain Biking Bend,* (Helena, MT: Falcon, 1998) provides detailed trail descriptions.

Finding the trail: From Bend, take the Cascade Lakes Highway (Forest Highway 46), 9 miles to FR 41. FR 41 is the first left turn after the Inn of the Seventh Mountain Resort. A half-mile down FR 41, turn left onto FR 4120. Follow the signs for 0.7 mile to the Lava Island Trailhead.

To reach the Benham Falls Trailhead, head south from Bend for 9 miles on U.S. Highway 97. Turn right at the signs for the Lava Lands Visitor Center. The visitor center has a sweeping view of the area and information on the area's geology. If you are heading to Benham Falls, turn left onto FR 9702,

The author after taking a dip in the Deschutes River.

just off US 97. Follow FR 9702 for 4 miles to the Benham Falls Picnic Area and Trailhead.

THE RIDE

After touring the Lava Island area, head upstream, following the bike trail signs. Follow the singletrack for 3.5 miles to Dillon Falls. Get on Forest Road 100 at Dillon Falls and ride the 3.4 miles to Benham Falls. From Benham Falls you can follow the bike trail over the Deschutes River to the Benham Falls Picnic Area. Return the same way or try some of the other roads between the river and FR 41.

Lower Deschutes River Trail

The mouth of the Deschutes River is only two hours from Portland; and this ride is a sure cure for the drizzle-induced blahs. The trail runs on the old Union Pacific railroad bed. Thorns and sharp rocks puncture many tires on this trail, so be prepared. The rough surface and long distance make this a moderately strenuous ride. Don't attempt this 32-mile ride during the occasional 110-degree heat of summer. The best time to visit is in winter or early spring when the orchards and wildflowers are blooming. Strong winds blow up and down the 2,000-foot deep canyon, making travel difficult. There are usually more people in boats on the river than on the trail. The trail passes several Class 3 and 4 rapids and gives anglers access to a productive section of the river. The winding canyons and immense vistas can swallow a person's feelings of importance without leaving a trace. Schedule enough time to visit Maryhill Museum, which is just across the Columbia from Biggs. The museum has a collection of Rodin's work that is one of the most sensual art collections in the Northwest. The Stonehenge replica near Maryhill is also an interesting visit.

General location:	The trailhead at the Deschutes River State Park is 100 miles east of Portland.
Distance:	32 miles, out and back.
Time:	5 to 6 hours.
Aerobic level:	Moderate, due to the long distance and rough surface.
Elevation change:	The trail climbs only 400 feet in 16 miles.
Tread:	Gravel railroad bed.
Technical difficulty:	3.
Hazards:	Rattlesnakes, dehydration, and flat tires are the main hazards. The snakes are rarely seen; bring plenty of water; and get puncture proof tires, if you can find them.
Season:	The trail is rarely closed by snow or ice, but summer days may be too hot to ride.
Services:	All services are available in The Dalles.
Rescue index:	Seek help in The Dalles.
Land status:	The trailhead is at the Deschutes River State Park; the trail is managed by the Oregon Parks and Recreation Department and the Bureau of Land Management.
Maps:	USGS: Wishram, Emerson, Locust Grove, Erskine.

Sources of additional information: Oregon Parks and Recreation Department; Bureau of Land Management, Prineville District.

Finding the trail: From Interstate 84, take Exit 97 at Cecillo or 104 at Biggs and follow old Oregon 30 west to the state park on the east bank of the Deschutes River. Parking for the bike trail is at the first parking area on the left, just off the old highway.

THE RIDE

The railroad grade maintains a constant 1 to 3 percent climb for 16 miles. While it seems flat when you start, the continuous climbing becomes exhausting.

LOWER DESCHUTES RIVER TRAIL

Ride 41

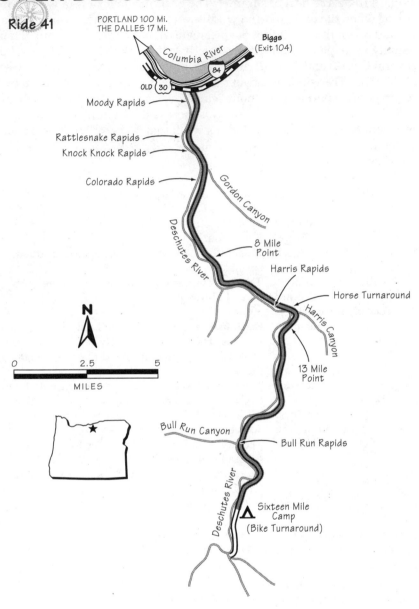

PORTLAND 100 Mi.
THE DALLES 17 Mi.

Biggs
(Exit 104)

Columbia River

84

OLD 30

Moody Rapids

Rattlesnake Rapids

Knock Knock Rapids

Colorado Rapids

Gordon Canyon

Deschutes River

8 Mile Point

Harris Rapids

Horse Turnaround

Harris Canyon

13 Mile Point

N

0   2.5   5

MILES

Bull Run Canyon

Bull Run Rapids

Deschutes River

Sixteen Mile Camp
(Bike Turnaround)

Heading toward Sixteen Mile Canyon on the Lower Deschutes River.

Less than 1 mile from the Columbia River, you pass the Class-III Moody Rapids. Rattlesnake Rapids, a Class IV, is 1.5 miles farther upstream. At 4 miles, you cross Gordon Canyon and pass the only other Class-4 rapid, the Colorado. The trail passes seventeen dispersed campsites between the Columbia River and Sixteen Mile Canyon. Seven of the campsites even have toilets, but they do not have drinking water. Bikes are prohibited beyond Sixteen Mile Canyon.

Davis Lake to Bobby Lake

The 10.6-mile climb to Bobby Lake starts amidst lodgepole pines on the edge of Davis Lake. In 1997, Davis Lake rose and covered most of Trail 99, which runs along the west edge of the lake. Over the last 10 years, mountain pine beetles have killed many of the lodgepole pines in the forest along the trail, and winter storms knock down hundreds of trees each year. When I road this trail in 1997, trees were strewn across the first 3 miles of the route, but by July 1998 the trail had been cleared. Trees will continue to fall. If the trail is blocked when you come to ride, start at the trailhead for Moore Creek Trail (40) off Forest Road

4652. Climbing over, around, and under fallen lodgepole is dangerous; the brittle branches cut and puncture skin easily. Call the Deschutes National Forest, Bend Ranger District, for more information (see Appendix).

The forest changes from lodgepole pine to fir and hemlock as you climb, so the number of downed trees diminishes. Bobby Lake is too cold for swimming, except on the hottest days, but you get a good view of the near-perfect cone of Maiden Peak from the lakeshore. Davis Lake has two campgrounds open to the public; they are located on the south side of the lake.

Families may find the 2.2 miles along Davis Lake on FR 650 more enjoyable than the tree-strewn trail. Park off the road near the gate. Road 650 is closed from January to August to protect wildlife.

Downhill thrill-seekers may want to try the 2.7-mile drop from nearby Maiden Peak on Trail 41. Don't plan on riding to the top of the 7,800 foot peak. The trail climbs over 1,500 feet in only 2.5 miles.

General location:	Davis Lake is 60 miles southwest of Bend.
Distance:	21.2 miles, out and back.
Time:	3 to 4 hours
Aerobic level:	Strenuous.
Elevation change:	The trail climbs 1,000 feet to reach Bobby Lake.
Tread:	Singletrack.
Technical difficulty:	4 and 5.
Hazards:	Downed trees may be plentiful and are dangerous to cross. Maintain control on the descent back to the trailhead.
Season:	June through October.
Services:	All services are available in Crescent and Bend.
Rescue index:	Seek help in Crescent or Bend.
Land status:	Deschutes National Forest, Crescent Ranger District.
Maps:	The Bend Ranger District Map provides good coverage of the area. The Forest Service also publishes individual trail sheets and brochures about mountain biking in Central Oregon. USGS: Davis Mountain, Hammer Butte, The Twins.

Sources of additional information: In Bend, several bike shops line the roads leading to Skyliner Road and the Cascade Lakes Highway. Many of the personnel in the shops are avid mountain bikers who are willing to share trail information.

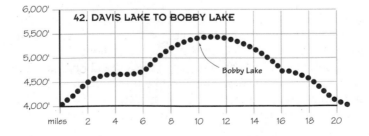

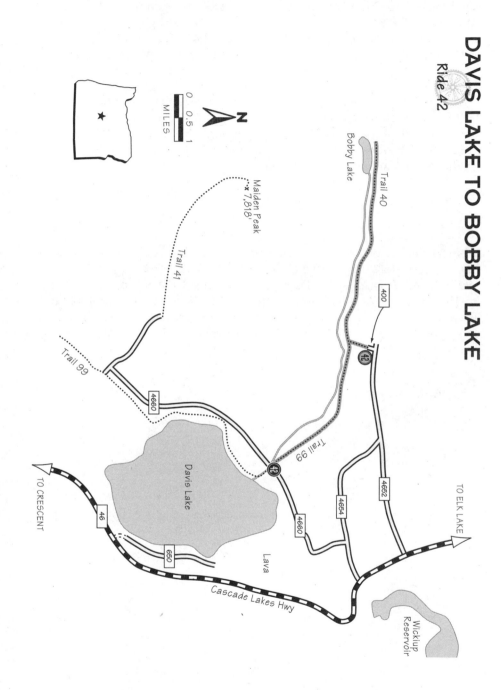

Finding the trail: The trailhead for starting near Davis Lake is on Forest Road 4660. Take Klamath County Road 61 from Oregon 97 in Crescent for 10 miles to Forest Highway 46, the Cascade Lakes Highway. Go north on the Cascade Lakes Highway for 11 miles to FR 4660, near the western arm of Wickiup Reservoir. Follow FR 4660 for 4 miles and park where Trail 99 crosses the road. Head east on the trail to get to Davis Lake; go west to reach Bobby Lake.

You can avoid most of the lodgepoles and reduce the length of the ride to 15.2 miles by starting at the trailhead off FR 4652. To reach this trailhead, go north on the Cascade Lakes Highway, 0.5 mile past the FR 4660 junction, to FR 4652. Turn west onto FR 4652 and follow it 3.5 miles to FR 400. The trailhead is0.5 mile up FR 400.

THE RIDE

If the trail is free of downed trees and water, take the short ride to the edge of Davis Lake before starting the climb to Bobby Lake. Trail 99 has a smooth, sandy surface for its first 4 miles. It passes through lodgepole pines as it heads up Moore Creek. At the junction with Trail 40 (Moore Creek Trail), the trail leaves the lodgepoles and enters fir and hemlock forest. The trail comes close to Moore Creek a couple of times in the 6.5 mile climb to the lake.

Southeast Oregon

Southeast Oregon's deserts stretch from the pine forests of the Cascades to the canyons of the Owyhee River near Idaho. Vast plains of sage flats and dry lakes are bordered by barren mountains and rugged canyons. The few remaining lakes attract tremendous flocks of waterfowl and have unique species of fish. The glaciated valleys on Steens Mountain and the alkaline lakes suggest that the area once had a much wetter and cooler climate. The locations and types of stone tools left by the earliest inhabitants indicate that this area had several alternating wet and dry climatic periods during the last ten thousand years. Ride 43 traverses the edge of the escarpment that is Steens Mountain and passes four glacier-carved gorges on the way to the 9,733-foot summit. The McCoy Ridge Ride (Ride 44) does not demand as much lung capacity as the ride to the top of Steens. It starts at an aspen-bordered lake in an alpine meadow and rolls gently down an open ridgeline on dirt roads. I learned that not all desert roads are as smooth as McCoy Ridge when I went looking for wild horses. What better place to look than Tombstone Canyon, along Burnt Car Road (Ride 45). Wild stallions mark their territory along the rough desert doubletrack with 2- to 3-foot-tall manure pyramids—stud piles. The tiny town of Frenchglen is a friendly place to gather provisions before or after an outing. It is a long drive to another town from this little hamlet.

Steens Mountain

Glaciers carved four immense, U-shaped valleys on Steens Mountain during the last ice age. This ride crosses the headwalls of all four valleys and reaches the summit of the highest mountain in Southeast Oregon. Most of the ride is above timberline, through alpine meadows and patches of snow. Wildflowers color the meadows throughout most of the summer. Aspens illuminate the landscape in fall. Some cyclists ride the entire 66-mile Steens Mountain Loop, starting in Frenchglen and climbing more than 5,000 feet. The ride described here includes some heart-pounding climbs and much of the breath-taking scenery of the loop road, but skips the hours-long desert crossing. Frenchglen lies at the south end of the marshlands that form the

Malheur National Wildlife Refuge. More than three hundred species of bird pass through the refuge every year; spring and fall are the best times to bird.

Bicycles must keep to the roads in the refuge. Taking the North Loop Road from Frenchglen, takes you past the P-Ranch. This was the headquarters for Pete French in the late 1800s when he ran the largest ranch in the U.S. The road crosses the Donner Und Blitzen River and climbs through sage and juniper desert for 16 miles before reaching Fish Lake. The aspen groves in the elevation band that includes Fish Lake indicate that the area receives more rain and snow than the surrounding desert. Some of the aspens bear initials of shepherds and hunters who visited the area 100 years ago. Golden eagles and bighorn sheep may be spotted along the cliffs on the east side of the mountain. Mirages and real lakes line the east side of the escarpment.

General location:	Steens Mountain is 20 miles east of Frenchglen.
Distance:	21.6 miles, out and back.
Time:	3 to 4 hours.
Aerobic level:	Strenous.
Elevation change:	The route starts at 7,370 feet and climbs to 9,773 feet before turning back.
Tread:	Two-lane gravel road.
Technical difficulty:	2.
Hazards:	Over-exertion leading to altitude sickness is a hazard on this ride. Take frequent breaks. The weather changes quickly and dramatically on the mountain. Be prepared for sudden lightning storms, snow, rain, and high winds.
Season:	The Steens Mountain Loop Road is usually open from July 1 to October 31. However, most of the road is free of snow and open to biking a week or two before the BLM opens the gate at Jackman Park. Call the Burns District BLM office to get the latest information on road openings.
Services:	Frenchglen has most services.
Rescue index:	This is a very remote area. Help may be available in Frenchglen, but the closest hospital is in Burns.
Land status:	Private land is interspersed with BLM and state lands. Stay on the roads.
Maps:	The USGS topographic map of Steens Mountain provides good coverage. The BLM's map of the South Half of Burns District provides adequate coverage for this ride and shows property ownership. USGS: Fish Lake, Wildhorse Lake.

Sources of additional information: Bureau of Land Management, Burns District.

Finding the trail: From Frenchglen, go east on the Steens Mountain North Loop Road. (The Steens Mountain Loop Road is officially divided into north and south portions, the dividing line being the top of Steens Mountain.) Fish Lake Campground is 16.5 miles from Frenchglen on the North Loop Road.

STEENS MOUNTAIN
Ride 43

McCOY RIDGE
Ride 44

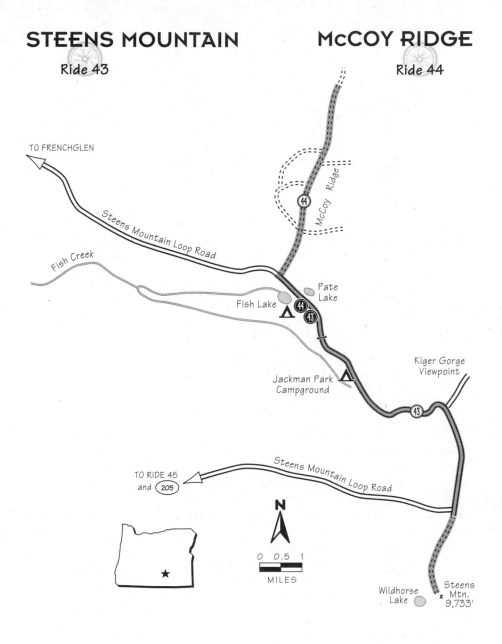

TO FRENCHGLEN

Steens Mountain Loop Road

McCoy Ridge

44

Fish Creek

Pate Lake

Fish Lake

44
43

Jackman Park Campground

Kiger Gorge Viewpoint

43

TO RIDE 45 and 205

Steens Mountain Loop Road

N

0 0.5 1
MILES

Wildhorse Lake

Steens Mtn. 9,733'

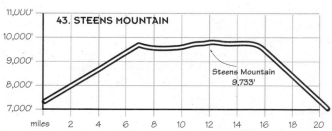

43. STEENS MOUNTAIN

Steens Mountain 9,733'

11,000'
10,000'
9,000'
8,000'
7,000'

miles 2 4 6 8 10 12 14 16 18 20

From the Fish Lake Campground, follow the North Loop Road for 6 miles to the Kiger Gorge Viewpoint Road. This segment is the most strenuous climb and passes Jackman Park gate and campground. Take the 0.4-mile detour to see Kiger Gorge, then return to the Loop Road. After 1.8 miles, the road passes the viewpoint for Little Blitzen Gorge. A mile past the Little Blitzen Gorge viewpoint a steep, 0.5-mile-long road on the left leads to the top of Steens Mountain (9,733 feet). The Loop Road veers right at a fork just past the road to the top of Steens Mountain. Stay left at the fork and ride 2.3 miles to the radio facilities. This section crosses the headwall of Big Indian Gorge and ends at the gated road leading to the radio facilities. Leave your bike at the gate—the last 0.25 mile to the radio facilities is too rocky to ride. Wildhorse Gorge and Wildhorse Lake lie beyond the end of the road. Return via the same route.

McCoy Ridge

This easy ride rolls in and out of aspen groves and along McCoy Ridge. The road passes a couple of shallow lakes and meadows, and it offers expansive views of the Blitzen Valley. This ride is a pleasant alternative to the arduous ride to the top of Steens Mountain. Several short spur roads lead east from the main road to hunters' camps and viewpoints. The more adventurous may want to try these side roads. The roads leading west go onto private land and some prohibit trespassing. Deer are plentiful. Local riders take this road to Krumbo Reservoir and Oregon 205.

General location:	On Steens Mountain, 16.5 miles southeast of Frenchglen.
Distance:	9.4 miles, out and back.
Time:	1 to 2 hours.
Aerobic level:	Easy, but remember you are at 7,000 feet elevation and over-exertion may cause altitude sickness.
Elevation change:	The road dips and rises while crossing several shallow valleys and gradually loses about 200 feet in elevation between Fish Lake and the turnaround point.
Tread:	Dirt road.
Technical difficulty:	2.

Southeast Oregon is dry and brown much of the year.

<table>
<tr><td>Hazards:</td><td>Hail, snow, rain, and lightning storms develop quickly. Riders should be prepared. Snow may fall on the mountain in the summer.</td></tr>
<tr><td>Season:</td><td>The road to Fish Lake is usually open from June 1 to October 31. Call the Burns District BLM office for road condition information.</td></tr>
<tr><td>Services:</td><td>Frenchglen has most services. Fish Lake Campground has potable water.</td></tr>
<tr><td>Rescue index:</td><td>Seek help in Frenchglen.</td></tr>
<tr><td>Land status:</td><td>Stay on the McCoy Ridge Road. Most of the land east of the road is private. The McCoy Ridge Road is open to the public.</td></tr>
<tr><td>Maps:</td><td>USGS: the 1:100,000 scale topographic map of Steens Mountain provides good coverage. 7.5-minute USGS quads: Fish Lake, Wildhorse Lake, and Big Pasture Creek. The BLM's map of the South Half of Burns District provides adequate coverage for this ride and shows property ownership.</td></tr>
</table>

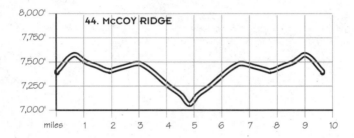

Sources of additional information: Bureau of Land Management, Burns District (see Appendix).

Finding the trail: Fish Lake Campground is 16.5 miles from Frenchglen on the North Loop Road. McCoy Ridge Road is 0.25 mile west of the campground and has a cattleguard near the intersection with the North Loop Road.

THE RIDE

Follow the road north for 4.7 miles. The turnaround point is at a gate and fence line on a hilltop.

Tombstone Canyon

This desert ramble through wild-horse country includes a visit to an abandoned homestead. The rock-lined spring and rock-walled house initiate thoughts of living in this lonely landscape. Obsidian flakes scattered near the homestead suggest that Paiutes used the spring long before the homesteaders. The coyote, wild horse, and deer tracks are evidence of who uses the spring most often today.

Near Tombstone Canyon, dozens of 2-foot tall manure pyramids (stud piles) mark stallions' territory and attest to heavy use by wild horses. The South Steens herd of three hundred horses has pitted the road with tracks.

The remote location requires that riders be prepared and able to read maps. The roads are not signed. There are numerous alternate routes in the area, including some shorter loops, but you increase your chance of seeing horses by getting away from the Steens Mountain Loop Road.

General location:	15 miles south of Frenchglen.
Distance:	22.2 miles, loop.
Time:	2 to 3 hours.
Aerobic level:	Moderate.
Elevation change:	This loop gains and loses fewer than 300 feet of elevation.
Tread:	Dirt, cobble, and gravel road.
Technical difficulty:	3.
Hazards:	Rattlesnakes are present, but dehydration and heat are probably greater hazards.
Season:	May to October; or when the Black Canyon Gate is open.
Services:	Frenchglen has most services.
Rescue index:	Seek help in Frenchglen.
Land status:	The route is on BLM land except for two small, private parcels crossed on road easements.
Maps:	The USGS 1:100,000 scale topographic map of Steens Mountain provides good coverage. USGS 7.5 minute quad: Roaring Springs Southeast. The BLM's map of the South Half of Burns District provides adequate coverage for this ride and shows property ownership.

Sources of additional information: Bureau of Land Management, Burns District.

Finding the trail: Take Oregon 205 10 miles south from Frenchglen to the Steens Mountain Loop Road. Travel east on the Loop Road to the second road on the left, approximately 2.4 miles from OR 205. The BLM map refers to this road as Burnt Car Road. Park off the road.

TOMBSTONE CANYON

Ride 45

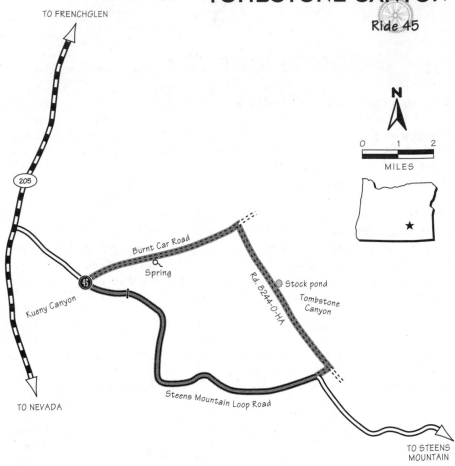

TO FRENCHGLEN

205

TO NEVADA

Kueny Canyon

45

Burnt Car Road

Spring

Rd. 8244-0-HA

Stock pond

Tombstone Canyon

Steens Mountain Loop Road

TO STEENS MOUNTAIN

N

0   1   2
MILES

★

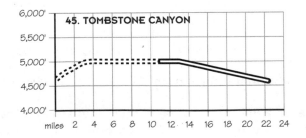

45. TOMBSTONE CANYON

6,000'
5,500'
5,000'
4,500'
4,000'

miles 2   4   6   8   10 12 14 16 18 20 22 24

THE RIDE

The trail starts with a moderate climb north of Kueny Canyon. The road is rocky, but the grade flattens after a mile. The road passes a rock-lined spring and the remains of a pumice-rock house at mile point 2.2, then heads through a pass to a broad valley running south to north. Shortly after emerging from the pass, turn right on the first road heading southeast. (The BLM labels this road 8244-0-HA.) This road runs along the base of juniper- and sage-covered rimrock for 2 miles before meeting a stock pond constructed on the stream leading into Tombstone Canyon. Continue to follow the road to the southeast. Approximately 2.5 miles southeast of the stock pond, you will be within 0.25 mile of the Steens Mountain Loop Road. Watch for the first jeep road on the right, which leads to the Loop Road. Take the Loop Road west to the trailhead.

The Blue Mountains

The Blue Mountain physiographic province includes the mountain ranges from the Maury Range and Ochoco Mountains, near Prineville, to the Wallowas near Idaho. The Blue Mountains are drier than the Cascades, but wet enough to grow pines and firs. The Blues are not as steep and rugged as the Cascades or Klamath Ranges. The trail riding is similar to that of Central Oregon, but most of the singletrack is in wilderness areas, and is therefore off-limits to bikes.

Some of the best rides are close to Prineville, in an area being managed for wildlife and recreation. Ride 46 runs the length of the Lookout Mountain Management Area. The road and trail loop is easier than going out and back on the trail. The shorter and easier Independent Mine Loop (Ride 47) is also in the Lookout Mountain Management Area. This 8-mile loop is short enough that you can do it twice; work on improving your technique the second time around.

The Round Mountain Trail (Ride 48) starts at the same trailhead as the ride to Independent Mine, but it heads north. The rolling terrain to Wildhorse Meadows on the north flank of Round Mountain is moderately strenuous. The ride from the meadows to the summit of Round Mountain is too difficult to bike up or down—at least it was for me. The Cougar Trail (Ride 49) was used by the Forest Service and miners from 1915 to 1922. This rugged trail along the northern boundary of the Ochoco National Forest climbs in and out of canyons and through logged and burned forests. The Forest Service thinned most of the stands, but a forest canopy still shades most of the trail.

The Hells Canyon defines the border between Idaho and Oregon. Riding down the Imnaha River Trail (Ride 50) to the Snake River will bring you to the border. The 7,000-foot deep gorge completely fills your vision as you ride along the Imnaha River. You have to climb the walls of the gorge to see the sky without straining your neck.

Lookout Mountain Trail

At an elevation of 6,926 feet, Lookout Mountain is the highest point in the Ochoco Mountains. Forests of ponderosa pine, Douglas-fir, white fir, and western larch cover the slopes. The Forest Service has been thinning and underburning some of the ponderosa pine stands over the last decade. The

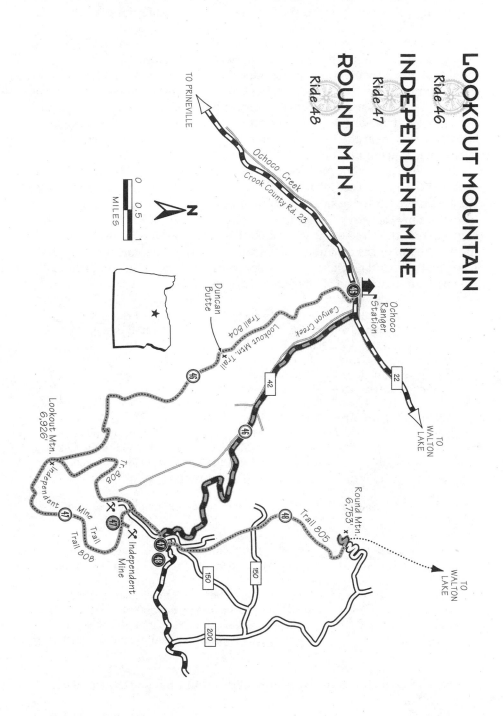

LOOKOUT MOUNTAIN
Ride 46

INDEPENDENT MINE
Ride 47

ROUND MTN.
Ride 48

TO PRINEVILLE

Ochoco Creek

Crook County Rd. 23

Duncan Butte

Lookout Mtn. Trail (Trail 804)

Ochoco Ranger Station

Canyon Creek

46

46

42

22

TO WALTON LAKE

Lookout Mtn. 6,926'

Independent Mine

Tr. 808

47

Independent Mine Trail Trail 808

47

47

48

48

Trail 805

150

150

200

Round Mtn. 6,753'

TO WALTON LAKE

N

MILES
0   0.5   1

burning reduces the risk of wildfire killing the old-growth pine and creates a pleasing park-like appearance. Elk are likely to be found grazing in recently burned areas.

Old-growth ponderosa pines are commonly referred to as yellow-bellies. Along the trail, you can see why—the massive boles of the pines have developed that golden tone. Many of the Douglas-firs are also hundreds of years old; growing on the cooler north-facing slopes, they have attained impressive size. A 0.5-mile-long ascent on the eastern side of Duncan Butte gives riders a brief rest from the long descent from atop Lookout Mountain. The steep rock-strewn section near the top of the mountain provides another break, since it is too dangerous to ride up or down.

Cascade peaks, from Mt. Hood to the Three Sisters, are visible from the grass- and sage-covered plateau on top of Lookout Mountain. To the east, the twenty-thousand-acre Big Summit Prairie creates a grassy hole in the forest canopy that stretches to the horizon. The Maury Mountains are to the south across the Crooked River Valley. The foundation of a former lookout marks the top of the mountain. The trail meets the Independent Mine Trail near the lookout. The Ochoco Snow Sports Snowmobile Club and Prineville Nordic Club maintain a shelter near the lookout site.

General location:	The trail is about 23 miles east of Prineville.
Distance:	18.5 miles, out and back on the trail or loop back on Forest Road 42.
Time:	3 to 4 hours.
Aerobic level:	Strenuous.
Elevation change:	2,947-foot gain.
Tread:	Singletrack for 12 miles and 6.5 miles on paved road.
Technical difficulty:	4.
Hazards:	The last 0.5 mile of trail west of the summit is on loose shale and jagged rock. Cliffs add to the risk of severe injury and convince most riders to walk portions of the trail. Control your speed during descents.
Season:	The trail is usually suitable for riding from mid-June to October.
Services:	Prineville has gas, food, and lodging.
Rescue index:	Seek help at the Ranger Station or in Prineville.
Land status:	Ochoco National Forest, Prineville and Big Summit ranger districts.
Maps:	Prineville and Big Summit ranger district maps provide the best coverage, but do not show the entire trail. USGS: Gerow Butte, Lookout Mountain. The Ochoco National Forest recreation map shows the trail.

Sources of additional information: Big Summit Ranger District, Ochoco National Forest.

Finding the trail: Take Oregon 26 east from the Ochoco National Forest Headquaters on the eastern end of Prineville for 15 miles and turn right on

Crook County Road 23. Take Crook CR 23, 8 miles to Ochoco Ranger Station. The trailhead and parking area is 100 yards east of the ranger station on the south side of the road. Start at this trailhead if you want to make the entire 3,000-foot climb at the beginning of the ride. To split the climb, start the ride at Forest Road 4205. Drive past the Ranger Station and turn right on FR 42. Continue on FR 42 for 6.5 miles to the top of the pass and the junction with FR 4205 on the right. Park at the trailhead marked for the Round Mountain Trail.

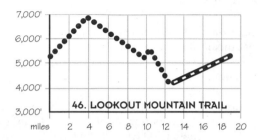

THE RIDE

The Lookout Mountain Management Area is closed to motorized vehicles, except in winter, when snowmobiles are allowed. For those seeking the most challenging route, start at the trailhead near the ranger station and ride the trail up and back. The 3,000-foot climb is almost continuous for 8 miles. You can also make a loop: ride the Lookout Mountain Trail to the summit, head north on Trail 808, and take FR 42 back to the trailhead.

A more reasonable approach is to split the climb into two sections by using a different trailhead. Start at the junction of Forest Roads 4205 and 42 (Ride 47 trailhead). Follow the Independent Mine Trail clockwise for 4.5 miles to the top of Lookout Mountain. Descend on the Lookout Mountain Trail and finish with a 6.5-mile ride back to the trailhead at FR 42.

See Map on Page 163

Independent Mine Trail

From this trailhead, the surprisingly easy climb to the top of Lookout Mountain passes so quickly you may want to do it twice in one day. The ride offers enough technical challenge to keep you focused, and the ascent exercises you without the punishment of riding the whole Lookout Mountain Trail (Ride 46). Mining cabins, shafts, and tailings give this ride historic interest.

Knowing that the forests and grasslands harbor wild horses, elk, bears, cougars, and coyotes keeps you alert to the sounds and movements around you. The explosion of feathers almost beneath your wheels is probably a ruffed grouse, which are common on the mountain. Less common, but even more startling, is the large gray goshawk that may dive at you if you are near its nest, then dart through fir thickets at incredible speed. Almost a third of the ride is on an open plateau that provides 360-degree views. Equestrians and hikers also use the trail, so control your speed on the descent. Use increases during hunting season.

General location:	The trailhead is about 30 miles east of Prineville.
Distance:	8 miles starting at Forest Road 42; or 6.2 miles starting at the end of FR 4205, loop.
Time:	1 to 2 hours.
Aerobic level:	Moderate.
Elevation change:	From the trailhead on FR 42, the trail climbs 1,500 feet. Starting at the trailhead 1 mile up FR 4205 cuts about 500 feet off the climb.
Tread:	Singletrack.
Technical difficulty:	4.
Hazards:	The Independent Mine extracted cinnabar, a red-colored ore containing mercury. Do not play on the mine tailings or venture off the trail near the mine. Be prepared for sudden changes in the weather.
Season:	The trail is suitable for riding when it is dry, usually June to October.
Services:	Gas, food, and lodging are available in Prineville.
Rescue index:	Seek help at the Ochoco Ranger Station or in Prineville.
Land status:	Ochoco National Forest, Prineville and Big Summit ranger districts.
Maps:	Prineville and Big Summit ranger district maps provide the best coverage, but do not show the entire trail. USGS: Lookout Mountain (does not show all the forest roads). The Ochoco National Forest recreation map shows the trail, so bring both the forest and district maps.

Sources of additional information: Big Summit Ranger District, Ochoco National Forest.

Finding the trail: From the Ochoco National Forest Headquarters on the eastern edge of Prineville, take Oregon 26 east for 15 miles and turn right on County Road 23. Take Crook CR 23, 8 miles to Ochoco Ranger Station. About 0.25 mile past the ranger station, turn right on FR 42. Follow FR 42 for 6.5 miles to the Round Mountain Trailhead parking area. The parking area is south of FR 42 and the trail begins on the western edge of FR 4205. You can follow FR 4205 for 1 mile to the other trailhead.

Starting at the Round Mountain Trailhead parking area, the sign pointing to the Independent Mine Trail is visible on the western end of the parking area near Forest Road 4205. The trail climbs parallel to FR 4205. You may lose the trail when it reaches a large, flat opening about 0.8 mile from the trailhead. Veer to the right and get on FR 4205, which takes you to the second trailhead.

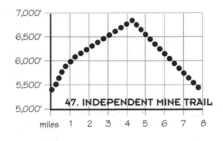

From the trailhead on FR 42, the trail, which is a cross-country ski route in winter, is marked with blue diamonds and ascends clockwise to the top. The counterclockwise route does not have blue diamonds. The clockwise route is a more gradual climb to the top of Lookout Mountain. The trail climbs gradually, dipping in and out of stands of fir, aspen, and pine before emerging on a sage and grass plateau at the top. Watch for the junction with the Lookout Mountain Trail. If you find you are nearing the western edge of a long ridge, you have missed the cutoff to complete the loop. The loop continues down switchbacks, through fir forests, and passes below the mine tailings.

See Map
on Page 163

Round Mountain Trail

The trail starts in open ponderosa-pine stands. The Forest Service has thinned most of the stands, but there are still a number of large pines and firs. Wild horses and elk benefit from the increased grass production in the thinned stands, which are less prone to fire than old-growth forests. While not usually considered a forest species, antelope also graze the lower slopes of Round Mountain.

The trail generally follows the ridgeline, and passes through several meadows and stands of old-growth fir and pine. Visitors usually hear the loud tappings and laughs of the pileated woodpeckers that inhabit the area. The last 0.4 mile of the route is on a steep gravel road. From the summit, the trail continues north to Walton Lake. The views from Round Mountain equal those from Lookout Mountain (Ride 46), which is to the south.

General location: The trailhead is about 30 miles east of Prineville.
Distance: 8.2 miles, out and back.
Time: 1 to 2 hours.

Aerobic level:	The first 3 miles are moderately strenuous. The ascent from the fenced pasture around Wildhorse Spring to the top of Round Mountain (6,753 feet) is extremely strenuous and requires advanced technical riding ability.
Elevation change:	The trail climbs 1,400 feet from the trailhead on Forest Road 42.
Tread:	Singletrack, except for 0.4 mile of gravel road near the top of Round Mountain.
Technical difficulty:	4.
Hazards:	Be prepared for sudden changes in the weather.
Season:	The trail is suitable for riding when it is dry, usually June to October.
Services:	Gas, food, and lodging are available in Prineville.
Rescue index:	Seek help at the Ochoco Ranger Station or in Prineville.
Land status:	Ochoco National Forest, Prineville and Big Summit ranger districts.
Maps:	Prineville and Big Summit ranger district maps provide the best coverage but do not show the trail. USGS: Lookout Mountain, Ochoco Butte (these maps do not show all the forest roads). The Ochoco National Forest recreation map shows the trail but not the local roads, so bring both the forest and district maps.

Sources of additional information: Ochoco National Forest, Big Summit Ranger District.

Finding the trail: Take Oregon 26 east for 15 miles from the Ochoco National Forest Headquarters on the eastern edge of Prineville and turn right on Crook County Road 23. Take Crook CR 23, 8 miles to Ochoco Ranger Station. About 0.25 miles past the ranger station, turn right on Forest Road 42. Follow FR 42 for 6.5 miles to the Round Mountain Trailhead parking area. The parking area is south of FR 42; the trail begins on the eastern edge of FR 4205.

THE RIDE

The trail drops from the parking area before crossing Forest Road 42. It runs below FR 150 for 0.5 mile before crossing it and heading up a ridge. The trail crosses FR 150 again at mile point 1.8. The trail is easy to follow at the road crossings. About 1.5 miles from the last road crossing, the trail enters the fenced pasture around Wildhorse Springs. From

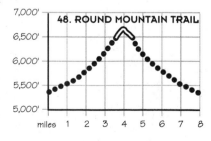

the fence to the top of Round Mountain, the trail climbs steeply on rocky tread. Just before reaching the summit, the trail hits FR 200. Follow the road the last 0.4 mile to the top. You will pass the trail to Walton Lake on the north side of Round Mountain near a switchback, about 0.1 mile from the summit.

Cougar Creek Trail

This trail follows the pack route used by miners and the Forest Service between 1915 and 1922. The Forest Service completed reconstruction of the trail in 1994. Many of the trees along the route bear the double scars of the first trailblazers. From several viewpoints along the route, riders will see that the desert starts on the parched south-facing slopes above Bear Creek. Riders pass juniper, mountain mahogany, and sage where the trail climbs over rocky ridges. Ponderosa pines and Douglas-firs fill the valleys. The temperature and humidity go up and down as the trail goes in and out of the canyons. The streams on this side of the Ochoco Divide flow north to the John Day River. Recent timber harvests have left slash over hundreds of acres along the trail; slash burning and windfalls may make passage difficult. Equestrian clubs have volunteered hundreds of hours to clear and mark this trail with wood yellow diamonds. Please be courteous to everyone you encounter.

General location:	The trail is about 27 miles northeast of Prineville, on the northern boundary of the Ochoco National Forest.
Distance:	16.4 miles, out and back.
Time:	3 to 4 hours.
Aerobic level:	Strenuous.
Elevation change:	Climbing in and out of Bear, Cougar, Dodds, and Heflin Creek canyons and several minor drainages, the trail has about 2,600 feet of total elevation gain and loss for the round trip.
Tread:	About 1 mile of the 8.2-mile trail is on logging roads. The singletrack portions are generally well maintained, thanks to equestrian clubs. Yellow diamonds mark the trail route.
Technical difficulty:	4 with some 5.
Hazards:	Be prepared for sudden changes in the weather. Rattlesnakes inhabit the rockier sections. The trail covers rocky terrain with cliffs.

COUGAR CREEK TRAIL

Ride 49

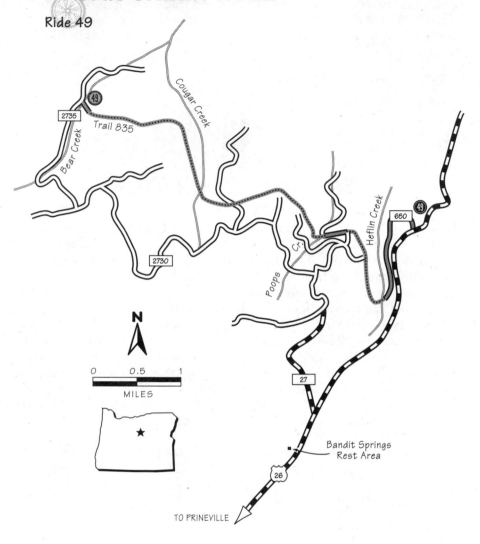

N

0   0.5   1
MILES

Cougar Creek

Trail 835

2735

Bear Creek

2730

Poops Cr.

Heflin Creek

650

49

49

27

Bandit Springs
Rest Area

26

TO PRINEVILLE

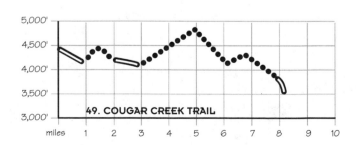

5,000'
4,500'
4,000'
3,500'
3,000'

49. COUGAR CREEK TRAIL

miles   1   2   3   4   5   6   7   8   9   10

Season: The trail is suitable for riding when it is dry, usually June to October.
Services: Gas, food, and lodging are available in Prineville and Mitchell.
Rescue index: Seek help in Prineville, Mitchell, or at one of the businesses near Ochoco Summit.
Land status: Ochoco National Forest.
Maps: Prineville and Big Summit Ranger District maps provide the best coverage, but do not show the trail. USGS: Lookout Mountain (does not show all the forest roads). The Ochoco National Forest recreation map shows the trail, so bring both the forest and district maps.

Sources of additional information: Ochoco National Forest, Prineville and Big Summit ranger districts.

Finding the trail: To reach the eastern trailhead, take Oregon 26 east for 27 miles from the Ochoco National Forest Headquarters, on the eastern edge of Prineville. Forest Road 650 is 2 miles past Ochoco Summit. The road is on the outside of a curve on OR 26. Watch for the brown road sign. Follow FR 650 around a small hill to the trailhead.

To reach the western trailhead, take OR 26 east from Prineville for 25 miles. Turn left on FR 27 (paved). After 1 mile, turn right on FR 2730 (gravel). Follow FR 2730 for 6.5 miles and turn right on FR 2735. Stay on 2735 for 1.5 miles, until it reaches a large dispersed camping area and the trailhead signs.

THE RIDE

(Described from the eastern trailhead.) Yellow wooden diamonds mark the trail and are especially helpful when the trail crosses roads. From Oregon Highway 26, the trail follows a logging road down to Heflin Creek. The major creek crossings have bridges, which are usually slippery. The trail climbs out of Heflin Creek canyon through one of the many thinnings and clearcuts on the route. When I rode the trail, the timber harvest areas on the eastern half of the trail appeared ready for burning. Hopefully, the trails will be cleared after the logging slash is burned. At times, the trail merges with a logging road in the Dodds Creek Drainage; follow the yellow diamonds and you won't lose it. The trail becomes rockier west of Cougar Creek. The last 0.25 mile of trail follows an old logging road to Bear Creek. Bear Creek does not have a bridge, but the numerous log jams and normally shallow depth allow easy crossing.

Imnaha River Trail

Most people traveling to this corner of the state want to see the Wallowa Mountains. Unfortunately for bikers, most of the mountains are in the Eagle Cap Wilderness, and are therefore off-limits to riding. A few trails and roads traverse National Forest land in the foothills of the mountains, but the best views may be from the county roads surrounding Joseph. In contrast, only a third of the 650,000-acre Hells Canyon National Recreation Area is wilderness, and some of the best trails are open to bikes. At 6,982 feet, Hells Canyon is the deepest gorge in North America. The depth of the gorge becomes apparent during the 3,000-foot descent to the trailhead from Joseph. The last 14 miles of the winding one-lane road to the trailhead are not suitable for passenger cars or those afraid of heights. Joseph has established a national reputation for bronze sculpture and several galleries in town display bronze art. The short trip along Wallowa Lake south of town should not be missed.

The Snake River, which is at the end of the trail, is fewer than 1,000 feet above sea level, so the climate at the bottom of the gorge is often surprisingly different from the climate in Joseph. The trail may be open even when Joseph is covered in snow. The trail runs along the west side of the Imnaha River to its confluence with the Snake River. People have lived in Hells Canyon for eight thousand years; the Nez Perce Indians raised thousands of horses on the grassy slopes of the canyon until they were chased out by the U.S. Army in 1877. The trail follows the Imnaha River as it winds through to a very rugged canyon. The trail ends at the site of a former mining town at Eureka Bar.

General location:	The trail is in the northeast corner of Oregon.
Distance:	8.6 miles, out and back.
Time:	1 to 2 hours.
Aerobic level:	Moderate.
Elevation change:	The trailhead is only 300 feet above the end of the trail at the Snake River, but it has several short climbs along the route.
Tread:	Singletrack.
Technical difficulty:	4; some sections of 5.
Hazards:	Rattlesnakes, poison oak, dehydration, and flat tires are the main hazards. The snakes are rarely seen; bring plenty of water; and get puncture proof tires, if you can find them. The narrow trail also has numerous steep drop-offs.
Season:	The trail is rarely closed by snow or ice, but summer days may be extremely hot.

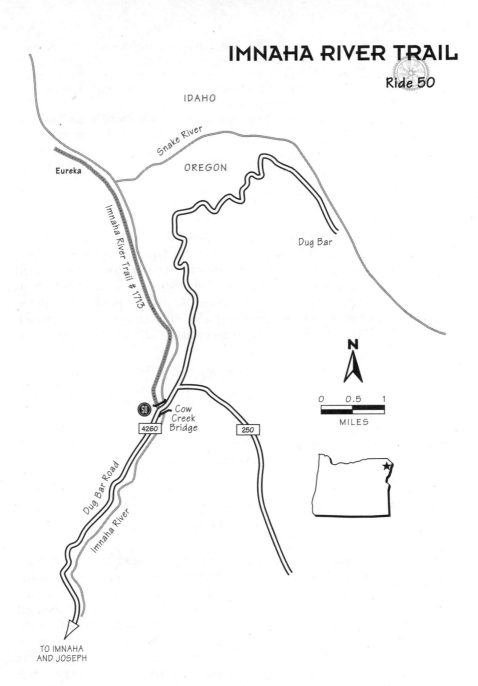

IMNAHA RIVER TRAIL
Ride 50

IDAHO

Snake River

OREGON

Eureka

Dug Bar

Imnaha River Trail # 1713

N

0   0.5   1

MILES

50

4260

Cow
Creek
Bridge

250

Dug Bar Road

Imnaha River

TO IMNAHA
AND JOSEPH

Services:	Imnaha has a store/tavern. Joseph has most services. Be sure to fill up with gas before leaving Joseph.
Rescue index:	This trail is very remote. The nearest help is hours away. Imnaha has a phone. Medical help is available in Enterprise.
Land status:	Most of the trail is in the Wallowa-Whitman National Forest, but it does cross a couple of private mining claims.
Maps:	The Wallowa-Whitman National Forest recreation map is adequate. The Hells Canyon NRA map is more detailed and displays topography. USGS: Cactus Mountain, Deadhorse Ridge.

Sources of additional information: Wallowa Mountains Visitor Center.
Finding the trail: Head west from Joseph on Oregon Highway 350 for 33 miles to the town of Imnaha. In "downtown" Imnaha turn left onto paved Wallowa County Road 735 and follow it down the Imnaha. After about 6 miles, the pavement ends and it becomes FR 4260 (Dug Bar Road), a steep, narrow road unsuitable for passenger cars and almost impassible when wet. The trailhead is 14 miles down this rough road at the bridge at Cow Creek.

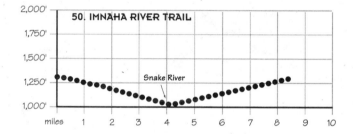

THE RIDE

If the dirt road is too rough, you may want to park along the county road and peddle the 14 miles to the trailhead. The trail was recently repaired and you can see where cliffs along the river had to be blasted to create the tread. The trail is on the west side of the river. The trail has some rocky sections and a few short climbs but generally descends at the same gradient as the Imnaha. It receives moderate to heavy use in the summer and during hunting season. The best time to ride it may be in the spring when wildflowers are in bloom and the mountain tops are still snow-covered. The canyon gets so deep and narrow that you may begin to imagine it is closing over the top of you. When you reach the Snake River Gorge, it is wide enough for you to see the sky again without dismounting to look up. The Eureka town site is along the Snake River and the old mines are visible on the hills above.

Appendix A

INFORMATION SOURCES

Nature of the Northwest Information Center (Recreation information for state agencies, national forests, and BLM districts)
800 NE Oregon Street
Portland, OR 97232

National Forests

Columbia River Gorge National Scenic Area
902 Wasco Ave., Suite 200
Hood River, OR 97631
503 668-1440
or 541-386-2333

Deschutes NF
Supervisor's Office
1645 Hwy. 20 East
Bend, OR 97701
541-388-2715

Fremont NF
Supervisor's Office
524 North G Street
Lakeview, OR 97630
541-947-2151

Malheur NF
Supervisor's Office
P.O. Box 909
John Day, OR 97845
541-575-1731

Mt. Hood NF
Supervisor's Office
16400 Champion Way
Sandy, OR 97055
503-668-1700

Ochoco NF
Supervisor's Office
3160 NE Third Street
Prineville, OR 97754
541-416-6500

Rogue River NF
Supervisor's Office
P.O.Box 520
Medford, OR 97501
541-858-2200

Siskiyou NF
Supervisor's Office
P.O.Box 440
Grants Pass, OR 97526
541-471-6500

Siuslaw NF
Supervisor's Office
4077 Research Way
Corvallis, OR 97333
541-750-7000

Umatilla NF
Supervisor's Office
2517 SW Hailey Avenue
Pendleton, OR 97801
541-278-3716

Umpqua NF
Supervisor's Office
2900 Stewart Parkway
Roseburg, OR 97470

Wallowa-Whitman NF
Supervisor's Office
1550 Dewey Avenue
Baker City, OR 97814
541-523-6391

Willamette NF
Supervisor's Office
211 East Seventh Avenue
Eugene, OR 97401
541-465-6521

Winema NF
Supervisor's Office
2810 Dahlia Street
Klamath Falls, OR 97601
541-883-6714

Bureau of Land Management

Burns District
HC 74-12533 Hwy 20 West
Hines, OR 97738
541-573-4400

Coos Bay District
1300 Airport Lane
North Bend, OR 97459
541-756-0100

Eugene District
2890 Chad Street
Eugene, Or 97408
541-683-6600

Lakeview District
1000 South Ninth Street
Lakeview, OR 97630
541-947-2177

Medford District
3040 Biddle Road
Medord, OR 97504
541-770-2200

Prineville District
3050 NE Third
Prineville, OR 97754
541-447-8800

Roseburg District
777 NW Garden Valley Blvd.
Roseburg, OR 97470
541-440-4930

Salem District
1717 Fabry Road SE
Salem, OR 97306
503-375-5646

Other Sources

City of Portland
Bureau of Parks and Recreation
1120 SW Fifth Avenue
Portland, OR 97204
503-823-6183

EE Wilson Wildlife Area
OR Dept of Fish & Wildlife
7118 Vandenburg Ave
Corvallis, OR 97330
541-757-4186

Oregon Parks and Recreation Department
1115 Commercial Street NE
Salem, OR 97310-1001
503-378-6305

Oregon Tourism Commission
775 Summer Street NE
Salem, OR 97310
800-547-7842

Oregon Department of Transprotation
Region 1
123 Flanders Street
Portland, OR 97209
503-731-8200

Crater Lake National Park
P.O.Box 7
Crater Lake, OR 97604
541-594-2211

Bonneville Lock & Dam
US Army Corp of Engineers
Cascade Locks, OR 97014-0150
541-374-8820

McDonald Forest
8692 Peavy Arboretum Road
Corvallis, OR 97330
541-737-4434 or
541-737-4452
www.cof.orst.edu/resfr

Appendix B

AUTHOR'S INDEX OF RIDES

Family Rides or Rides for Beginners

1 Barlow Road (most sections), Gate Creek to Government Camp
3 Springwater Corridor: Portland to Gresham
4 Springwater Corridor: Gresham to Boring
6 Forest Park: Springville Road Loop
7 Banks/Vernonia State Park
10 Bayocean Peninsula
14 Eagle Creek Overlook to Bonneville Dam
15 Hood River to Mosier
16 Sandy River Delta
18 Indian Ridge/Shining Lake Trail
21 Opal Creek
22 Willamette Mission State Park
23 E. E. Wilson Wildlife Area
24 Row River Trail
28 OC & E Woods Line State Trail: Bly to Klamath Falls
32 Eagle Rock Loop
41 Lower Deschutes
44 McCoy Ridge

Great Climbs

1 Barlow Road: Gate Creek to Government Camp
11 Mary's Peak
43 Steens Mountain
46 Lookout Mountain Trail, Number 804
48 Round Mountain Trail, Number 805

Great Downhills

2 Pioneer Bridle Trail
11 Mary's Peak
25 Dunning Ranch
39 Phil's Trail, Number 24.5
46 Lookout Mountain Trail, Number 804

Abundant Wildlife

10 Bayocean Peninsula
23 E. E. Wilson Wildlife Area

25 Dunning Ranch
28 OC & E Woods Line State Trail: Bly to Klamath Falls
43 Steens Mountain Trail, Number 804

Wet Weather Rides

3 Springwater Corridor: Portland to Gresham
4 Springwater Corridor: Gresham to Boring
6 Forest Park: Springville Road Loop
7 Banks/Vernonia State Park
10 Bayocean Peninsula
12 McDonald Forest, roads not trails
13 Tanner Creek Road
14 Eagle Creek Overlook to Bonneville Dam
15 Hood River to Mosier
16 Sandy River Delta
18 Indian Ridge/Shining Lake Trail
20 Mollala River, Huckleberry Trail only
21 Opal Creek
22 Willamette Mission State Park
23 E. E. Wilson Wildlife Area
24 Row River Trail
25 Dunning Ranch
27 Crater Lake
28 OC & E Woods Line State Trail: Bly to Klamath Falls
29 OC & E Woods Line State Trail: Woods Line Branch
41 Lower Deschutes
43 Steens Mountain
44 McCoy Ridge

Technical Riding Challenges

8 Gales Creek
9 Nels Roger–University Falls Loop Trail
20 Mollala River, Huckleberry Trail only
25 Dunning Ranch
26 The North Umpqua Trail: Tioga Segment
38 Lava Lake to Sparks Lake, Trails 4 and 99
42 Davis Lake to Bobby Lake
49 Cougar Trail, Number 835

About the Author

Mark Wigg has worked and played in Oregon for twenty years. He has fought fires, tracked owls, and, for the last fifteen years, he has taken great pleasure in exploring Oregon's wilderness on his mountain bike. He has reported on environmental impacts and published recreation guides to ten of Oregon's thirteen national forests. He currently works for the Oregon Department of Transportation as an environmental project manager.

get FALCON GUIDED

FALCON GUIDES® are available for where-to-go hiking, mountain biking, rock climbing, walking, scenic driving, fishing, rockhounding, paddling, birding, wildlife viewing, and camping. We also have FalconGuides on essential outdoor skills and subjects and field identification. The following titles are currently available, but this list grows every year. For a free catalog with a complete list of titles, call FALCON toll-free at 1-800-582-2665.

BIRDING GUIDES
Birding Minnesota
Birding Montana
Birding Texas
Birding Utah

FIELD GUIDES
Bitterroot: Montana State Flower
Canyon Country Wildflowers
Great Lakes Berry Book
New England Berry Book
Pacific Northwest Berry Book
Plants of Arizona
Rare Plants of Colorado
Rocky Mountain Berry Book
Scats & Tracks of the Rocky Mtns.
Tallgrass Prairie Wildflowers
Western Trees
Wildflowers of Southwestern Utah
Willow Bark and Rosehips

FISHING GUIDES
Fishing Alaska
Fishing the Beartooths
Fishing Florida
Fishing Glacier National Park
Fishing Maine
Fishing Montana
Fishing Wyoming

PADDLING GUIDES
Floater's Guide to Colorado
Paddling Montana
Paddling Okeefenokee
Paddling Oregon
Paddling Yellowstone & Grand
    Teton National Parks

ROCKHOUNDING GUIDES
Rockhounding Arizona
Rockhound's Guide to California
Rockhound's Guide to Colorado
Rockhounding Montana
Rockhounding Nevada
Rockhound's Guide to New Mexico
Rockhounding Texas
Rockhounding Utah
Rockhounding Wyoming

WALKING
Walking Colorado Springs
Walking Denver
Walking Portland
Walking St. Louis

HOW-TO GUIDES
Avalanche Aware
Backpacking Tips
Bear Aware
Leave No Trace
Mountain Lion Alert
Reading Weather
Wilderness First Aid
Wilderness Survival

MORE GUIDEBOOKS
Backcountry Horseman's
    Guide to Washington
Camping California's
    National Forests
Exploring Canyonlands &
    Arches National Parks
Exploring Hawaii's Parklands
Exploring Mount Helena
Recreation Guide to WA
    National Forests
Touring California & Nevada
    Hot Springs
Trail Riding Western
    Montana
Wild Country Companion
Wild Montana

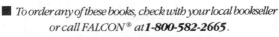

■ *To order any of these books, check with your local bookseller
or call FALCON*® *at* **1-800-582-2665**.
Visit us on the world wide web at:
www.falconguide.com

FALCON®

get
FALCON GUIDED

SCENIC DRIVING GUIDES

Scenic Driving Alaska and the Yukon
Scenic Driving Arizona
Scenic Driving the Beartooth Highway
Scenic Driving California
Scenic Driving Colorado
Scenic Driving Florida
Scenic Driving Georgia
Scenic Driving Hawaii
Scenic Driving Idaho
Scenic Driving Michigan
Scenic Driving Minnesota
Scenic Driving Montana
Scenic Driving New England
Scenic Driving New Mexico
Scenic Driving North Carolina
Scenic Driving Oregon
Scenic Driving the Ozarks including the
     Ouchita Mountains
Scenic Driving Texas
Scenic Driving Utah
Scenic Driving Washington
Scenic Driving Wisconsin
Scenic Driving Wyoming
Back Country Byways
National Forest Scenic Byways
National Forest Scenic Byways II

HISTORIC TRAIL GUIDES

Traveling California's Gold Rush Country
Traveling the Lewis & Clark Trail
Traveling the Oregon Trail
Traveler's Guide to the Pony Express Trail

WILDLIFE VIEWING GUIDES

Alaska Wildlife Viewing Guide
Arizona Wildlife Viewing Guide
California Wildlife Viewing Guide
Colorado Wildlife Viewing Guide
Florida Wildlife Viewing Guide
Idaho Wildlife Viewing Guide
Indiana Wildlife Vewing Guide
Iowa Wildlife Viewing Guide
Kentucky Wildlife Viewing Guide
Massachusetts Wildlife Viewing Guide
Montana Wildlife Viewing Guide
Nebraska Wildlife Viewing Guide
Nevada Wildlife Viewing Guide
New Hampshire Wildlife Viewing Guide
New Jersey Wildlife Viewing Guide
New Mexico Wildlife Viewing Guide
New York Wildlife Viewing Guide
North Carolina Wildlife Viewing Guide
North Dakota Wildlife Viewing Guide
Ohio Wildlife Viewing Guide
Oregon Wildlife Viewing Guide
Tennessee Wildlife Viewing Guide
Texas Wildlife Viewing Guide
Utah Wildlife Viewing Guide
Vermont Wildlife Viewing Guide
Virginia Wildlife Viewing Guide
Washington Wildlife Viewing Guide
West Virginia Wildlife Viewing Guide
Wisconsin Wildlife Viewing Guide

FALCON®

■ *To order any of these books, check with your local bookseller*
*or call FALCON® at **1-800-582-2665**.*

Visit us on the world wide web at:
www.falconguide.com

get FALCON GUIDED

MOUNTAIN BIKING GUIDES
Mountain Biking Arizona
Mountain Biking Colorado
Mountain Biking Georgia
Mountain Biking New Mexico
Mountain Biking New York
Mountain Biking Northern New England
Mountain Biking Oregon
Mountain Biking South Carolina
Mountain Biking Southern New England
Mountain Biking Utah
Mountain Biking Wisconsin

Local Cycling Series
Fat Trax Bozeman
Fat Trax Colorado Springs
Mountain Biking Bend
Mountain Biking Boise
Mountain Biking Chequamegon
Mountain Biking Denver/Boulder
Mountain Biking Durango
Mountain Biking Helena
Mountain Biking Moab
Mountain Biking the White Mountains (West)

FALCON®

■ *To order any of these books, check with your local bookseller
or call FALCON® at* **1-800-582-2665**.

Visit us on the world wide web at:
www.falconguide.com

get
FALCONGUIDED

BEST EASY DAY HIKES SERIES
Beartooths
Canyonlands & Arches
Best Hikes on the Continental Divide
Glacier & Wateron Lakes
Grand Staircase-Escalante and the Glen Canyon
    Region
Grand Canyon
North Cascades
Olympics
Shenandoah
Yellowstone

12 SHORT HIKES SERIES
Colorado
Aspen
Boulder
Denver Foothills Central
Denver Foothills North
Denver Foothills South
Rocky Mountain National Park-Estes Park
Rocky Mountain National Park-Grand Lake
Steamboat Springs
Summit County
Vail
California
San Diego Coast
San Diego Mountains
San Francisco Bay Area-Coastal
San Francisco Bay Area-East Bay
San Francisco Bay Area-North Bay
San Francisco Bay Area-South Bay
Washington
Mount Rainier National Park-Paradise
Mount Rainier National Park-Sunrise

■ *To order any of these books, check with your local bookseller*
or call FALCON® at **1-800-582-2665**.

Visit us on the world wide web at:
www.falconguide.com

FALCON®

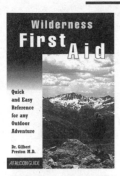

WILDERNESS FIRST AID

By Dr. Gilbert Preston M.D.
Enjoy the outdoors and face the inherent risks with confidence. By reading this easy-to-follow first-aid text, all outdoor enthusiasts can pack a little extra peace of mind on their next adventure. *Wilderness First Aid* offers expert medical advice for dealing with outdoor emergencies beyond the reach of 911. It easily fits in most backcountry first-aid kits.

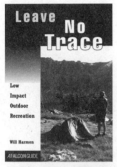

LEAVE NO TRACE

By Will Harmon
The concept of "leave no trace" seems simple, but it actually gets fairly complicated. This handy quick-reference guidebook includes all the newest information on this growing and all-important subject. This book is written to help the outdoor enthusiast make the hundreds of decisions necessary to protect the natural landscape and still have an enjoyable wilderness experience. Part of the proceeds from the sale of this book go to continue leave-no-trace education efforts. The Official Manual of American Hiking Society.

BEAR AWARE

By Bill Schneider
Hiking in bear country can be very safe if hikers follow the guidelines summarized in this small, "packable" book. Extensively reviewed by bear experts, the book contains the latest information on the intriguing science of bear-human interactions. *Bear Aware* can not only make your hike safer, but it can help you avoid the fear of bears that can take the edge off your trip.

MOUNTAIN LION ALERT

By Steve Torres
Recent mountain lion attacks have received national attention. Although infrequent, lion attacks raise concern for public safety. *Mountain Lion Alert* contains helpful advice for mountain bikers, trail runners, horse riders, pet owners, and suburban landowners on how to reduce the chances of mountain lion-human conflicts.

Also Available
• ***Wilderness Survival*** • ***Reading Weather*** • ***Backpacking Tips***
• ***Climbing Safely*** • ***Avalanche Aware***
To order check with your local bookseller or
call FALCON® at **1-800-582-2665.**
www.falconguide.com